You probably think this song is about you

You probably think this song is about you

Kate Camp

TE HERENGA WAKA
UNIVERSITY PRESS

Te Herenga Waka University Press
Victoria University of Wellington
PO Box 600, Wellington
New Zealand
teherengawakapress.co.nz

A catalogue record is available at the National Library of New Zealand.

ISBN 9781776920129

Published with the support of

Printed in Aotearoa New Zealand by Your Books

Contents

You probably think this song is about you

I loved to sit on my own and sing. The section behind us was empty, filled with fennel as tall as we were. Between our house and the section was the volley board, painted the only colour brown that things seemed to be painted then, a mid brown, a bit orangy. I could sit on the ledge at the back of the volley board, putting my feet on the concrete block wall, and there, hidden from view, outdoors but in complete privacy, I would sing over and over again the song I considered the most beautiful and heart-rending and profound: 'The Streets of London'.

We were not a musical family. We had a piano, and Mum could play the theme to *Hill Street Blues*, but she didn't much. My sister did the recorder. The sound was banal but the instrument itself seductive, like a sculpture made of milk chocolate. My father had a clarinet. I remember the case it was in, putting the segments together and taking them apart, wedging them into their green velvet voids. I can feel the silver pieces under my fingertips, the way they were cushioned against the body of the clarinet, and smell the bottle of oil that was kept in there, along with the brush for cleaning. But I never heard it make a sound.

Our parents didn't have a lot of records, and the ones they had they didn't really listen to. There were the two Beatles double albums—the red one and the blue one—and *Sergeant Pepper*, and *Blood on the Tracks*. There was the Simon and Garfunkel with Paul Simon in a stripy top. And there was *Joseph and the Amazing Technicolor Dreamcoat*, with the jean jacket covered in badges. It was *Joseph* that I listened to over and over, lying on my stomach on our Nile green carpet, with the golden yellow lyrics sheet, its corners worn to a softness like fabric, the smoked-glass square of the record compartment, and the architecture of the underside of the dining table above me like some looming shipworks.

The clever rhymes and witticisms I found in songs filled me with admiration and envy: *Always wanted to be an apostle, knew that I would make it if I tried. Then when we retire, we can write the Gospels, so they'll still talk about us when we've died.* I am swinging on the swing at our beach house at Waikanae. It's a hollow, green plastic seat, attached with yellow rope to a timber frame that's built out from the house. It's evening, the heat has gone out of the day, Dad is behind me somewhere, getting the barbecue going, the smell of methylated spirits and the invisible flame on the charcoal. I'm swinging and singing that song over and over, *Look at all my trials and tribulations*, and it all builds to the cleverness of those lines, of that rhyme of apostle and gospel, and I know it's irreverent about religion, which, even though we're a family of atheists in a secular world, I still get a kick out of. And Dad walks past and sings *Always wanted to be an opossum*. I am both slightly hurt that he has sullied the beauty of the song, and impressed enough by the joke to store it away for later use.

More than any other, the lyric which obsessed me as a child was the chorus of 'You're So Vain'—*You're so vain, you probably think this song is about you. You're so vain, you probably think this song is about you.* I remember turning that over and over in my head: she's saying he's vain, because he thinks the song is about him, but the song is about him . . . It was like a Zen koan, a perpetual motion machine, something that, no matter how much you thought about it, you couldn't solve, because it meant both things at the same time. And it appealed to me too, how she turned her hurt feelings into something funny, and even though the song was all about him, it was really all about her, because she was the clever one, the one who rhymed *yacht* with *apricot*, and said *clouds in my coffee* which didn't make sense but sounded fantastic.

There were many things in childhood which we enjoyed, but needed to pretend we hated. Singing in school assemblies was one of these. We would sit cross-legged on the dusty wooden floor of the hall looking up at the words on the overhead, neatly written out with *V1* and *V2* and *Chorus* in the margin in red. Our school music in the 1970s was in a kind of transition. In throwback mode, we danced to 'Jump Jim Crow' in folk dancing, and sang 'My Grandfather's Clock', changing it of course to 'My Grandfather's Cock': *It was taller by half than the old man himself, though it weighed not a pennyweight more.* Then there were the cool songs, the domain of our music teacher Mr Carpenter, who had big curly hair and a moustache. He got us to sing 'Crazy Little Thing Called Love', which had only just come out. I may be making this up, but I think we were even snapping our fingers in time.

Mr Carpenter was the only male teacher at our school, and he was a different generation to the other teachers, more like one of the students from *Fame*. When I got the role of narrator in our production of *Winnie the Pooh*, the three of us—Pooh, Christopher Robin and I—went round to Mr Carpenter's on a Saturday to practise our lines. He offered us a cup of coffee and I can remember the mug it came in, which seemed oversized, but then again, I was only ten. He had a packet of Oddfellows on the coffee table—the bag had been torn open and was lying there with the Oddfellows exposed, like dusty pieces of a fallen temple. I had only ever seen lollies offered from the neatly opened top of a bag, or poured into a bowl for a party. That Oddfellows bag, torn open with such abandon, the rubber plant growing in the corner, the huge mug with the little specks of instant coffee that had floated to the top: the height of sophistication had been reached.

Actually, there was another male teacher at our primary school, Mr Tichborne, immortalised in the Pool Rules: *No Running. No Ducking, No Diving* and—in green crayon—*NO TICHBORNES*.

God knows who was in charge of the music repertoire of my intermediate, but imagine the sound of several hundred eleven- and twelve-year-olds singing the theme from *M*A*S*H*: 'Suicide Is Painless', how we could take or leave it if we pleased. So haunting, and you couldn't help but picture as you sang the faded, bleached-out credits of the TV series, the helicopters coming over the dry hills, the army doctors holding their hats as they ran into the dust—that strangely serious opening for a comedy, which even had a different light, a different colour palette, from the programme itself.

Gradually I became aware of music as tribal, a way of belonging, a signal of social status. For the first time there were musicians I'd heard of rather than just songs I knew. Singers might appear as removable pin-up posters in our *My Guy* magazine. Along with Scott Baio and Ralph Macchio there might be Leif Garrett or Andy Gibb. I have a memory of standing in a group, being part of a conversation about music, and hoping no one realised I didn't know the difference between Bruce

Springsteen and Rick Springfield.

It was around this time that Mary got her first radio, or *transistor radio* as we called it. She was allowed to stay up to listen to *The Top Ten at Ten*. I hated that radio. It was yet another thing that she could lord over me. And when I did get my own, it still wasn't the same, because I didn't really enjoy listening to it. I wasn't actually that interested in *The Top Ten at Ten*. But learning the words to songs was something that we all did as girls. Girls knew the words. We would tape *American Top 40 with Casey Kasem* and play songs back over and over, trying to decipher tricky phrases, then write the lyrics down on a pad of Basildon Bond note paper—the thin, lined kind, not the good kind Mum used for writing to Argentinian dictators. I would like to say that I learned the words to good songs, but the ones I remember learning were things like 'Industrial Disease' or Kid Creole and the Coconuts' 'Stool Pigeon'.

I still know the words to so many songs, am amazed at how they will arrive unbidden in my mouth, songs I haven't thought of or heard for decades, songs I didn't know I knew, songs I actively despise, like 'I've been to paradise but I've never been to me'. And I have that memory for poems too, and for music. I sing in a choir where everyone else reads music but I have to learn it all by ear and there are arrangements from years ago, parts I'm sure I've forgotten, but we start to sing and there they are, in my body, where they've been lodged the whole time. And maybe I've always been like that, because there's a story from my early life which takes place in the chemist in Khandallah. I'm nine months old, a baby in my mother's arms, and a woman behind Mum in the queue says, 'Your baby can hum the whole of "Oh My Darling, Clementine".' Or I was three months old. Or it might have been my sister not me. But it was Clementine *In a cavern, in a canyon, excavating for a mine.*

I wet
my pants

When we were growing up, there were hardly any clothes shops for children. The only one I recall was Susan and Samuel, which had a sister store called Edward and Emma. I can't remember which one of them was in the Khandallah village, but I wet my pants in whichever one it was. The details are hazy, just my mother's exasperation—*The toilets are right there!*—and that feeling of wet pants and trousers, how it's warm at first, and it's a relief to stop holding on, but then it goes cold and clammy almost immediately. Clothes shopping itself was a humiliating activity, fraught with self-consciousness and things left unsaid. Tall and gawky with short hair and glasses, I was always being mistaken for a boy, which I hated, but I hated it so much that I couldn't admit I hated it, and so could never suggest growing my hair, or wearing girlier clothes. I expect that contributed to the pants wetting—I was out of my element, and in front of a strange adult, a clothes shop woman, a type I always found made me feel even more awkward than usual.

To wet your pants at six or seven is one thing, but in the next memory I have I was definitely too old, perhaps just turned eleven. We went away on a sports trip to Hawke's Bay, and were billeted. I used to stay at my grandma's all the time, and occasionally at the houses of friends I knew well, but staying at the house of a strange family was another level of social challenge. I send love to the mother of that family for the dinner she made: the table was set with bread, hard boiled eggs, grated carrot, cheese, ham, all in separate bowls for us to help ourselves. None of the dreaded unfamiliar foods that can be served up, in huge portions, at the houses of people you don't know. I remember a meal of "fish pie" served up by one of our neighbours that had the consistency and colour of porridge—it was pie in name only, no pastry just the blob of grey-white filling. They were an old-fashioned family, a strict family, and I picture the mother with a scarf on her head, though I may be making up that detail to accord with the wartime austerity of the meal.

So the mother of my billet family was obviously lovely, and I'm sure the girl I was billeted with was too. I even have a vague memory of them showing me the toilet, and it being like a public toilet, with a silver door that only went two thirds of the way down, but that detail doesn't make any sense. Anyway, I was in the girl's room, *busting to go loo* as we would say, but too shy to ask,

15

until from under the stool I was sitting on there was the pattering sound of wee hitting the carpet, and even then, when it was so obvious, I said something like *Oh, I must have spilled my drink bottle* . . . I can't remember what happened next. I've got no doubt that my billet mother dealt with it in a very no-fuss way. But today, at forty-five, it is still hard to bring myself to write that line about the drink bottle. The cover-up may not be worse than the crime but it is, somehow, even more humiliating.

Our own mother was an absolute terror on urination. Like any sensible mother of the time she always made us go before we went anywhere: *And squeeze out every last drop!* But she loved to torment us when we were on our way home in the car. If you told mum to hurry because you needed to go to the loo she'd say *Niagara Falls! Niagara Falls! Great gushing rivers!* and go *pssssssssss* all the way home. Then you'd be at the door, bent over double, trying to get the key in the lock while behind you she'd be invoking rivers, lakes and waterfalls. There was a toilet just inside, the red toilet, so-called because the seat was red, along with the red wallpaper with baskets of black and white daisies. You'd always wee your pants a little bit, trying to get the sliding door open.

The next time I pissed myself I was twenty-five. It was some months after my friend Mark had killed himself, and I was spending a weeknight at home with a friend in the usual way, sitting in front of the fireplace in the bedroom of my flat, smoking joints, chain-smoking

Port Royal roll-your-owns, and drinking instant coffee. I'd never been a huge drinker, but I'd taken to keeping a hip flask in my room, and having capfuls of brandy along with the dope, which I'd been finding wasn't as effective as usual at taking the edge off my emotions. I got up to make a coffee, walked into the kitchen of the flat. The only sensation I had was of a microsecond passing, like a blink of the eyes, but suddenly I was in another world. I looked around the unfamiliar landscape, mystified. Where the hell was I? In front of me was a vast plain, like the Serengeti at dawn, pale pink and utterly flat like a desert. In the distance were undefined shapes—maybe bison or wildebeest? Then I looked beyond them and saw sheer, dramatic cliffs, dark brown and shining, rising up precisely vertically from the plain. I was filled with a sense of wonder, rather than panic, a David Attenborough-esque awe at the majesty of nature. Then I became aware of a dull ache in my left cheek. Looking harder at the cliffs, I realised they were the legs of a 1970s wood and basket-weave armchair. The African plain was the pastel carpet. The wildebeest, balls of fluff and dog hair. I had passed out on the living-room floor.

I got up, went into my bedroom, and told my friend she had to go. The next day I looked up drug and alcohol counselling in the phone book and made an appointment to see someone at NSAID, the National Society of Alcohol and Drug . . . something. The counsellor I got was called Marta; she was from somewhere like Bulgaria and had a flat, pretty face, with a hare lip. It made her look a bit like a moon in a book of nursery rhymes, and I remember thinking *I don't think this woman's going to be able to help me.* She did though, and I successfully stopped smoking dope for a while. But fast forward some months, I'm out with a group, including the brother of my dead friend. We'd been corresponding since the funeral—by letter, how quaint!—and I think we both knew we were going to get together, although it was a terrible idea for all the obvious reasons and some less obvious ones too. But anyway, we're out with a group, and I'm smoking dope again after months on the wagon, and I'm drinking heavily, and then we're back at my place, and I suppose I pass out for a moment while he's out of the room, and when he comes back in I find I've wet the bed. I try to pass it off as a spilled glass of water. We both know that isn't what's happened, but we kind of play along to keep the peace. We just flip the mattress over and sleep on the other side.

I remember when I moved out of that flat, how I looked at that room from the doorway once it was empty. It was a great flat, far nicer than anywhere a student would normally live: Dad had bought it when I went back to university after dropping out, the kind of gold-plated second chances I would benefit from all my life. The flat occupied the middle story of a rambling Arts and Crafts house, and my room was huge, with oak-panelled walls painted cream, polished wood floors, tiny-paned windows looking down the valley onto greenery, and a working fireplace with a purple-tiled surround. The house was built below street level, and sometimes, on a still night, you'd hear voices coming down the chimney from people walking past outside. I used to scavenge firewood from building sites on my way home from university, carrying offcuts of four-by-two in a bag on my back like an insect as I laboured the way up the hill on my bike. I wrote my first book in that flat, sitting up late at my desk, smoking and writing with the reflected room in the windows in front of me. I wrote my university essays there and came home with exciting As and occasional annoying Bs. And I made affirmations for myself—I remember on the door having a sign that said *1995 a year to thrive a year to drive a year to enjoy just being alive.* I didn't actually start driving until 1996 but, you know.

Looking at the room when it was empty, I realised how much sadness I'd felt in it. There was so much going on at the time when Mark killed himself. I was angry and guilty, yes, but I was also full of bravado, I was pedalling as fast as I could to keep ahead of how I was feeling, I was succeeding like I never had before, but I was ashamed and greedy and ugly and needy and, as they say in the Bible, like a dog returning to its vomit, I was a fool returning to my folly, going back to my dope, and back to my messed up bully of a boyfriend to get the dope, time and time again. It was a surprise to feel the simple sadness of the empty room, a feeling of a different order, almost noble. And I registered something like compassion for myself, which was in short supply in those days. I felt sad for what that girl had gone through, the girl who picked up the phone in the office of her first real job, and a woman she didn't know said *I'm afraid I've got some terrible news*. And so even the fireplace with its purple tiles and magical voices I was glad to put behind me.

When I moved to Johnsonville in my thirties, to be near my sister and her new baby, it was the first time I'd lived within sight of the golden arches. You could tell yourself the flat was OK: it had good sun, polished floors, it was upstairs so you could see, not just McDonald's, but suburbia around you on one side and Johnsonville Mall on the other. The smell of the previous tenant's meat fat, of the white residue of chops cooked and the pan left out overnight in the minuscule kitchen, was the kind of thing that not everyone would notice, but I am particularly sensitive to smells and of all the awful things about that place it is that meat fat smell that I remember best. If I tell you the other three things that were terrible I won't need to explain them: I was living above two seventeen-year-olds; I had recently suffered a break-up; and I couldn't get the internet going. *We are experiencing unusually high call volumes and the average waiting time is two hours and forty-five minutes.*

I don't recall the night as having been anything particularly outlandish. After a function with an open bar, a work friend and I had headed to Courtenay Place. I was drunk enough to buy cigarettes although I 'wasn't smoking' at the time—who knows how long a stretch I destroyed on that night out. We sat outside in the cold so I could smoke, drinking red wine by the glass and talking shit. I remember being drunk enough to need to concentrate when ordering every second two glasses of pinot noir, that moment of performance as you make studied eye contact, articulate your order, and manage your card and the EFTPOS machine. I would have taxied home, again enunciating my address with careful concentration. By this stage, I had moved from the spacious front bedroom because of the noise that came from my downstairs neighbours. I was sleeping in the back room, which was barely big enough for my double bed, and on that bed I had an extraordinary blanket which I'd bought at Pauanesia in Auckland: knitted peggy squares, made from unravelled jerseys. It is really too heavy to sleep under, so heavy that your feet can't stay upright but are pushed to one side or the other. At some point I must have put on the electric blanket—like all New Zealand flats, it was freezing in winter.

When I woke, I'd wet the bed, and the electric blanket was still on full. I had the kind of head you get from red wine, cigarettes, and hours of overheating. It was a beautiful sunny winter's day, extravagantly bright. I dragged the mattress into my living room, poured vinegar on the piss in some kind of recovered household hints memory. I drank some water and had some Panadol and made a cup of tea. And I sat there at the kitchen table, in my dressing gown and sunglasses, shaking with hangover, and cried. That kind of shame, the shame that comes when you are not coping and you can't tell anyone, is so inexplicable when you're not feeling it. I think I would have been more willing to tell my friends, my family, that I had wet the bed, than that I had sat and cried at my table. Of course I didn't do either; I let my mattress dry out in the sun and it didn't seem to suffer many aftereffects. I showered in the bathroom with its mouldy trim between the bath and the wall, and its odd, mysterious smell of plastic bags.

That afternoon I was supposed to be going along to a singing group that I'd heard about. I was already part of the Wellington Community Choir, which had upwards of 100 people, singing in parts, and that had given me the confidence to try out this other group, which met on Sundays sometimes and was run by Bryan Crump. I didn't really know Bryan, he was the friend of a friend, but he'd said if I liked singing I should come along. It would have been so easy not to go, I had every reason. I remember looking at the glass-fronted bookcase which had come from my father's office. It was made of dark wood, and the glass door on each shelf opened upwards with two round silver knobs, and slid back, like the compartments for cakes and sandwiches in an old-fashioned coffee lounge.

When you think about rock bottom, it sounds like a one-time thing, but in my experience it's a place you end up going to over and over again. If you're lucky, you learn something each time you visit. At this rock bottom, I sensed that this singing group could be an important thing for me, a way of keeping faith, perhaps, with my childhood self, who loved more than anything to sing. As sick and ashamed as I was feeling, I knew that if I didn't go I would feel even worse.

I don't remember what we sang, but it was the first time I'd ever experienced the kind of a capella arrangements where you just go *ooh ooh la la la* in all different places, instead of singing the words all together. That whole concept was new to me, and it was pretty terrifying. But when I think about that day in Bryan's living room in Graymor Flats, I feel such a sense of gratitude. No one there knew me, or knew that I'd woken that morning on the fringes of Johnsonville's suburban shopping centre, with a mouth like some Dantean cavern, trapped under the world's heaviest blanket in an overheated bed soaked in my own piss. I said to Bryan later that it was nice of him to ask me to join the group. He must have known through our mutual friend that I had been through a tough break-up, and thought it might do me good. 'No,' he said, 'I just needed another alto.'

I've just remembered the one other time I wet my pants as an adult. Given it happened in the middle of the morning, in the central business district, with no alcohol involved, I'm surprised it had slipped my mind. I've always been prone to urinary tract infections, the main symptom of which is an irresistible, overwhelming urge to urinate. The sense of urgency is impossible to convey if you haven't experienced it—that feeling of being right on the precipice of pissing yourself at any second makes you so panicky, it's like being an adrenaline-charged prey animal caught out in the open.

In this state, I left my work in Bowen Street for an external meeting at a café on the Terrace. I can't recall who with or what about, all I remember was that I drank a lot of water, couldn't concentrate, and went to the toilet three times in the half hour I was there. The meeting ended, and I decided I couldn't go back to the office, I'd have to get a taxi and go home. I walked gingerly towards the cab stand at the top of Woodward Street, but all that water I'd drunk was catching up with me, and suddenly I knew that I couldn't make it home, or back to the office, I couldn't even make it to the taxi. It was a crisp autumn day on the Terrace, I was the Director of Communications for the Ministry of Economic Development, and I was about to wet my pants like a three-year-old.

I turned into the nearest office building, looking for a stairwell that might, god willing, contain a toilet. By some miracle the stairwell door was unlocked, but even as I put my hand on the handle I felt the piss soak down my grey woollen tights, and as I ran up the stairs I could hear the pat pat pat as drops of it hit the lino. There was, thank god, a women's toilet off the stairwell's first floor, and I got myself into a cubicle, but there was no way I could get my tights down in time. I should have been horrified, but you know, the body is a powerful thing, and instead I was almost elated with relief as the urine ran down my legs and onto the cubicle floor. Assessing my options, the situation was actually better than I could have imagined. I'd left the office without my jacket, wearing an airforce-blue, needle-cord shirt dress, tights, and khaki patent leather heels. The tights were soaked, but the dress was unscathed, and once I'd tipped out the shoes (!) they looked fine. Mopping up the floor with toilet paper, and leaving my tights and underwear in the rubbish bin, I strode out of the building with purpose. With bare legs the outfit was actually quite glamorous, and the two waiting taxi drivers gave each other a look as I hopped into the front car.

Sometimes I feel like humiliation is the most powerful force in the universe. Years, decades, lifetimes later, you can still bring it to mind, and go red, and sweat and feel shame. Where other emotions can fade away, even disappear, so no matter how hard you try you can't feel them anymore, and sometimes can't even remember how it felt to feel them, humiliation seems to survive. Maybe it's protected by its very privacy and secrecy. It never fades, because it's kept from the light.

My grandfather was ten years old when his mother

died. She'd had cancer, I think, but no one talked about cancer then, and he hadn't known it was coming, just came home from school one day and it had happened, and he was sent round to an aunt and uncle's. The day of the funeral, he was wearing an outfit he'd never worn before, he told me. It had trousers with elaborate button flies, and afterwards, at the wake, he wet his pants. 'I didn't know how to manage the buttons,' he said. 'Mum wasn't there, and I didn't know who else to ask.' His voice got rough, and he hit his chest with a fist, in a gesture that I somehow knew was what he did when he was trying to stop himself crying, even though I'd never seen him cry before. 'There weren't anyone else I could ask.' He pronounces 'ask' the Yorkshire way, even though it's more than sixty years since he moved to New Zealand, and more than eighty since he ruined his good trousers on the day of his mother's funeral.

Izard Road
and Oliphant Place

Grandma and Grandpa's house was at Oliphant Place, which was obviously a good thing because it sounded like elephant. So many things were different in Hastings. It was always sunny. It was very flat, so that when you drove past the railway crossing, whichever adults were in the car would need to say that it was *the highest hill in Hastings*. In winter you'd get a frost that would put ice on the top of a bucket of water and make the towels go stiff on the line. At Oliphant Place there were a grapefruit tree and a feijoa tree and a passionfruit vine on the back of the garage, and the next door neighbours had a mandarin tree. That house ended up burning down, and Grandma and Grandpa had to put the hose onto the horribly burned neighbour. A child died. They didn't know that family well. In earlier times they knew all their neighbours in Oliphant Place, and we would visit their houses, maybe my sister and I would hold hands and sing 'Any Dream Will Do' from *Joseph and the Amazing Technicolor Dreamcoat*, or maybe we would just go to look at Mrs Treacher's collection of hundreds of shoe ornaments, glass ones and china ones and a pair of wind-up sneakers that walked across the table on their own. Grandma had found these very entertaining, and asked at a shop in town whether they had any wind-up toys for adults, not children. The shop assistant went into the back storeroom and brought out a vibrator.

The first smell of Grandma and Grandpa's house isn't the house at all, it's the smell of their car, and I smell it sometimes when I get into cars now, the smell of an immaculately clean, well-maintained car that has been parked in the baking sun with the windows up. Maybe there's a hint of woollen picnic rug in there too. The kind of car that if you open the glove compartment will have just the owner's manual, a box of tissues, and an open bag of Mint Imperials. I was wriggling on Grandma's knee in the front seat one time, kicking her in the shins, and she slapped me on the leg. When she was hanging the washing out later, I went out and solemnly asked *Do you shoot people too Grandma?* Mum had extremely liberal views on corporal punishment.

You never get out of Grandma and Grandpa's car in the garage, because there isn't really room to open the doors. The garage is tiny and neatly stored against its walls are sun umbrellas, camp beds, old spring bed bases, pieces of wood, and other things that give it a gloomy, functional, satisfyingly garagy smell.

The front steps at Grandma and Grandpa's are famous because of a black-and-white photo of Mary cracking walnuts there with a hammer. She's probably four years old, and I think she has some kind of kerchief around her hair, is wearing an apron, and looking at the camera with such a look of glee, because she's saying *Put your finger here Grandma.* The sweet taste of fresh walnuts, so much more satisfying for having been cracked open, is one of the many flavours that I associate with Hastings, and by *Hastings* I mean, of course, not the provincial city, but my Grandparents' house, their neighbours' houses, and the handful of places we might visit while we were there: Fantasyland, the swimming pool, Frimley Park with its open grass and English trees.

The door to Grandma and Grandpa's has those hanging plastic strips on it, to keep the flies out. You enter into the sunroom which is tiny, there's just Grandma's sewing table, and a cupboard, and maybe the vacuum cleaner is stored in there, then you're in the kitchen, which has a number of fascinating, old-fashioned things in it: a *meat safe* and a stove you light that burns little pieces of wood, so that when you get up in the morning, and you're sitting on a stool squeezed in at the table-height kitchen bench in your flannelette nightie and poodle-cloth dressing gown, waiting for your cooked breakfast, Grandma is opening a little door at the front of the stove and feeding in pieces of wood, and you can see flames in there. She is cooking on a fire. Breakfast at Grandma and Grandpa's consists of, depending on the season, half a grapefruit sprinkled with sugar or a dozen or more feijoas, then Grandma's homemade muesli, then poached eggs on toast, then toast with jam, and a mug of Milo made with milk. Most likely a glass of bright yellow freshly squeezed grapefruit juice too, with the squeezed-out grapefruit halves piling up in a bowl in the kitchen sink as Grandpa squeezes them with the metal squeezer, bringing the handle down again and again.

If you eat in the kitchen, you're eating on plates and bowls that are dark brown with a red flower pattern on them, and whenever I see that china now it reminds me of food my Grandma made: stew with mashed potato, served in a bowl so you could stir it all together, or custard, which she always called *tustard*, and with their Yorkshire accents that they never lost it was *toosterd*, like the vowel sound in *book*. Their accent was always a source of family stories. My uncle, raised in New Zealand by Yorkshire parents, came home from his first day of school outraged to announce *It's lunch, not loonch!*

Also in Grandma and Grandpa's kitchen is the biscuit tin with the racehorse Cardigan Bay on it, and there must be other biscuit tins too, because Grandma always has multiple types of biscuits, cakes and slices on hand: Madeira cake and chocolate cake, ginger biscuits and peanut biscuits and caramel fudge (foodge) and shortbread (yawn) and, if it's Christmas, chocolate

30

cherry fudge, made with red and green glacé cherries of which the story will inevitably be told, in the marvelling tones of a miracle, of how one time the melted chocolate base revealed the word still, somehow, intact: *Cadbury*. The cupboards have those silver latches on them that you poke your finger into to open. In the kitchen drawer, shockingly, is a packet of cigarettes. They are Grandma's, although she doesn't smoke, hasn't for years, not since her youth in the war when everyone smoked. But they're there. The only other object of interest I can remember from that kitchen is an address book, the kind where you move the little triangle up and down the alphabet, then press a button, and it flips open at that letter. I am absolutely certain I have been told to stop playing with it. Was it in this kitchen that a jar of peaches exploded while Grandma was bottling, spraying my father with boiling hot syrup and broken glass and, with no car, necessitating a trip to the hospital on the back of Grandpa's bicycle? Not sure. Maybe that was their first house in Hastings, with the dirt floor, and the mice, and the milk kept in a basin of water under a wet cloth, so that when Grandma experienced her first earthquake she saw the water ripple and shake.

The living room is through the kitchen door. It gets expanded at some point, but originally it's just got room for a small sofa, and the dining table pushed against the wall, and an armchair, and the coal-look electric fire with its tiled surround, and the glass paperweight

31

with coloured-glass things in it like sea anemones, and a convex mirror, and a succulent plant on the windowsill, and some ginger jars on the pelmet, with patterns of Japanese blossoms. And there's the *pouffe* which is a dark mustardy velvet, with a cushion on a metal base with a skirt around it, and at some points in life you're small enough to hide under there, and then later it's a good place to look for Easter eggs, and then, later, it will be so hard to believe that the person who used to be able to fit into that tiny space is you, that the same person can inhabit two such different bodies and still remember what it was to be in the other, tiny body. And the TV's in the living room, in the corner by the fire, and if you have to go to bed half an hour early because you're the youngest, before *CHiPs* starts, even though your parents let you stay up and watch it at home under a special exception, you can creep silently out of your bed and sit in the hallway and watch *CHiPs* through the crack in the open door. No one knows you're there because you get away with it every time.

If you're not watching TV, you might be playing Chinese Checkers, the satisfying feeling of the pegs fitting into the softened neat-fitting holes of the thick cardboard, or Pick-up Sticks, down on the floor, looking at the pile from an inch off the carpet, from every angle, trying to work out how to get the black one out, which is worth 50, and if you're the youngest and have that personality, sometimes you might take your chances and just throw the whole pile into chaos, because you're sick of it taking so long, and having to be so careful, and no one getting anything out. Or maybe you're playing the version of Pick-up Sticks where it's all tiny garden implements: a tangle of tiny cream-coloured spades and forks and rakes.

When Grandma and Grandpa moved to a retirement village, my uncle packed up the house. He asked if we wanted anything, and what I wish I'd thought of, what I really wish I had, is the soap holder that was in their bathroom. It was orange, made of plastic, in the shape of an oval with a line through the middle, and on each side were spikes, on one side holding the soap, on the other holding the thing itself off the basin—that way your soap doesn't make the basin messy, and it lasts longer. There was a great sense of satisfaction that came from putting the soap down on the soap rack, or picking it off, and seeing the little holes that it had in the bottom, and also in putting the soap aside for a minute, and washing the soap dregs off the holder, the caked-on pieces around the little spikes, and then washing down the soap too, so that it was smooth and perfect again—a *cake* of soap, Lux or Knights Castile. We never use soap now, we use handwash, but I wish I had that soap holder.

We lived with Grandma and Grandpa for three months, the year I turned seven, while Mum and Dad travelled in Europe. Grandpa taught us how you can tie your dressing gown belt like a tie, and how you can dry yourself with just a flannel. First you wipe the drips off yourself with your hand, then you dry yourself with the flannel, wringing it out tightly when it gets wet. It was something he did in the war. I do it that way for a while. When Mum and Dad come back, Mary and I ignore them and go out to the garden to play. I have worked out some trick questions to ask them, to check if they are our real parents, or robots made to look like our parents. I ask them our dog's name, and where we keep the back door key. We don't have a back door, just a front door and a side door. They say, *We don't have a back door; we keep the side door key under the garden fork.* So I know it is really them.

Grandma and Grandpa's bedroom is in the cool corner of the house, with the feijoa tree outside the window making everything seem green. There's built-in wardrobes and a dressing table, and Grandma has her *cold cream* there, and other things that she smells of. In the morning, we go into Grandma and Grandpa's bed and play eye spy. There's the same small number of things to guess each time, the same ornaments lined up along the pelmet: the wooden flying fish and painted coconut, souvenirs of Pitcairn Island. The ship stopped there when Grandma and Grandpa and Dad emigrated to New Zealand, so the islanders could row out and sell things. There are more ginger jars, because Grandpa loves his ginger, and there's a huge shell, with mother of pearl inside, and a tiny yellow lamb, an inch high. It's made of beads strung onto elastic, and when you push the bottom of the little black base it sits on the lamb collapses, and when you let the base go it springs back up again. When you're in bed with Grandma and Grandpa, there's always the chance they will do plu-plums on you, which means a big pinch on your bottom. And they will say Yorkshire things like *get away with you* or *cheeky moonkey*. Grandma and Grandpa's bed has a quilt on top of it—I'm sure Grandma sewed it herself, it's green on the back, and on the top it's a bluey sea-green, some kind of silk that looks different colours in the light. The edge has a ruffle, and there's an oval-shaped pattern sewn into the middle. It's filled with feathers, and sometimes one will work its way out through the material, and you'll pull it out and it will be like a whitecap on the ocean. We have that quilt on our bed now, in the summertime, *the Grandma and Grandpa duvet* we call it. It's older than I am. *You think you feel old*, Grandpa said to me once, *try having a granddaughter that's forty*.

Grandma's house was called *Izard Road* because that's how you refer to houses, you say the name of the street but you mean a particular house, and by that you mark a particular era. When I went to Grandma's with my family we went through the front door. The front door was green with a panel next to it of glass that had tiny raised dots. I can feel them under my fingers now, the braille of them, and I can hear the sound they make when you run your fingernail over them. On the porch would be Grandma's gardening gumboots, ankle high, with a trim of some kind of fur.

Most of the time I went to Grandma's on my own, and I came through the back door, down the concrete steps by the garage, past a hydrangea bush, and into Grandma's place via the laundry. My Grandma, my Aunty Carole and my cousin Nigel lived there together, and I was round there all the time—after school, even before school sometimes to have breakfast on my way. It was the house I knew best after our own, the house where I could climb out the window, or sit on the hot-water cylinder, or roll myself up in the dark green circular rug, see the world with its fringes hanging down. And now I want to go back and walk through those rooms again.

Grandma would be sitting at the dining table, doing the crossword, or the Target, with the words in her distinctive handwriting piling up in the margin of the newspaper. I am sitting at the table, wriggling around in my seat, talking to Grandma who is looking at me and laughing. She was quite deaf, with a whistling hearing aid, and probably had no idea what I was saying half the time, but that would have been fine, because I would happily just talk and talk, and eat of course, because there was always things to eat at Grandma and Carole's that were treats, that we would never have at home, like a cold chicken leg in the fridge, or a bottle of Fanta in the fridge door.

There's a table cloth on the dining table, and the silver salt and pepper shakers. I have them now on my kitchen bench—a *salt cellar* I want to say, if that's the right spelling of that word. And on the wall above the dining table is a print of Van Gogh's *Sunflowers*, which I know Grandma likes because you can see the name *Vincent* written on the vase, and that was my Grandfather's name who died when I was little and I don't remember.

Grandma's got an orangy yellow canary in a cane cage. I can't remember its name, only the name of the concrete sparrow next to its cage, which is called Sally, the name of my Uncle Adrian's ex-wife, Grandma's ex-daughter-in-law. They lived in America most of my life so I never knew them. She's never said anything, but I know that Mum doesn't really approve of having a concrete sparrow named after your son's ex-wife. There are some things where Mum and my Grandma and Aunty Carole don't see eye to eye.

Grandma has a sofa in her house which is called a Chesterfield. I don't know why. It's big and blue–green, and when I stay the night, which I quite often do on a Friday, I sleep in the lounge on the sofa cushions on the floor, made up with sheets like a real bed. And when I stay the night we might have tomatoes on toast for dinner, on white bread with mayonnaise and salt and pepper, and we'll watch *That's Incredible* with Fran Tarkington and Cathy Lee Crosby, and then Carole and Grandma and I will stay up late and eat Black Knight liquorice, so much that it will make my poo go dark greeny black, and we'll watch *Entertainment Tonight*, which doesn't come on until ten o'clock. *Da da da da da da*, that's the theme of *Entertainment Tonight*, I'm getting a real Proustian kick out of singing that aloud right now. Of course these days you can go on Youtube and listen to the theme songs of all your old TV shows, the opening bass notes of *Barney Miller*, or the tune of *Benson*, the clever Black butler.

So that my cousin Nigel can have a room of his own, Grandma and Carole share a room. A few times I've slept in there too, sharing my Aunty's single bed. *Having Catherine in the bed is like having an electric element in the bed* she says and I feel secretly proud of the fact that I am a hot sleeper. Carole found it annoying when Grandma picked her toenails in bed at night. It was probably something she mentioned once, but now, forty years later, with my grandmother dead for decades, I always think of her when I pick my toenails, and I feel a sense of affinity, like we are occupying the same body. *I get a shock when I look in the mirror because I don't feel different than I did when I was eighteen*, I remember Grandma telling me once. The whole thing was very abstract, because I was probably only ten myself, so being eighteen and being really old like Grandma were both hard to imagine. Another time she told me *You'll be gorgeous when you're seventeen*. It was an awfully long way away.

Grandma loves gardening, and she loves flowers and she does ikebana which means putting an interesting-shaped branch into a vase on her coffee table. She holds these in place with spiked metal things that sit at the bottom of the vase, like a bed of nails. A smell I always associate with my Grandma is garden rubbish being burned in the incinerator. Is she in her nightie and a dressing gown, and her garden gumboots, pushing branches down into the incinerator with a rake? The sound I associate with her is the sound of the push mower, the whirring slicing of the blades.

Grandma is very small, and her name is Dorothy, or Dot. Sometimes she puts her hair in curlers. One time she says to me that instead of a shower, you could just wash with a flannel on your face and neck and between your legs. *Between your legs!* I am shocked that she would mention such a thing. Once, her neighbour Mrs Noble got horribly injured and there was a lot of dripping blood. Once the woman next door got stabbed or attacked in some way. Maybe that was the dripping blood. These are things I don't get to really hear about, but they're always there, in the periphery of my Grandma's house, like the garage, which is up on the street and filled with my aunty's furniture. A couple of times I get to go in there and see it, with an Aladdin's cave sense, sun coming in through a high window and things stacked up so it's hard to move around.

I like writing poems on people's birthdays, in their birthday cards, and one year my Grandma writes one for me, on the envelope:

Hail to the Blythe Spirit just turned twelve!
The words not mine I had to delve.
Floats through the door and greeting 'Hi!'
Darting round and looking for some 'kai'.
Chat of work and mates and eyes aglow
Then rings her mum and yells, I gotta go!
Up pack, up coat, up scarf and then
—out the door, this lanky, bubbly, gorgeous Catherine.

I did always have a scarf in winter. It was a long
skinny one knitted by mum, in oatmeal-coloured wool.

A packet of
Benson and Hedges
and a box of matches

The Fisherman's Table is on the road between Wellington and Waikanae. Stopping there for dinner was one of those treats that might occur on our way to the beach for the weekend. The Fisherman's Table had a salad bar that was in a boat; you could have as much as you wanted. They always brought slices of white bread and butter to the table as soon as you sat down. There was a small bar attached to the restaurant. It was darker than the rest of the place, with an underwater glow—was there a fish tank in there with one of those purple lights? That was the feeling of the place. Mary and I might go there after dinner and have a Shirley Temple which was red lemonade. Or we might go out and wait in the car, while Mum and Dad stayed in the restaurant for a drink.

We would sit in the front seats not the back, and we would take cigarette butts from the ashtray, the long ones, maybe they'd been put out halfway or just burned out through neglect. We'd push in the cigarette lighter, its green ring of light, wait for it to pop, and then draw it out, the glowing spiral of its metal interior the only light, and we'd 'smoke' the cigarette butts, or at least light them, seeing for the first time how flecks of tobacco would stick on the lighter surface, burning brightly for a second before disappearing.

As two sisters in the back seat, there was something very right about driving with Mum and Dad. It was a metaphor, I guess, for our lives: kids and adults together, in two separate though connected worlds. Mum and Dad had the front seats. They had the radio, with those black buttons you would push for preset stations. In the back we could close our eyes and try to guess where we were by the corners. When you opened your eyes it took a second to recognise the familiar street, because you'd been so certain you were somewhere else.

In the front seat they had all the power. They knew things, about the Bible and the Table of Elements, things in *Time* magazine and the *Bulletin*. They could do things that we couldn't: they could drive and smoke and drink, they could lick knives, snap their fingers and whistle. And yet, on some level, we looked down on them. There were many things about their adult world that we utterly disdained. The way they would fold up a small amount of toilet paper neatly, instead of bunching up a big handful. How they drank black coffee in the heat of summer. The boringness of their life, with its droning sound of the

National Programme coming from the leather-cased Sanyo that Mum would even put in the laundry basket when she went to the washing line. And we disdained their smoking, of course, even as we enacted its rituals.

In my next memory of cigarettes, I am probably eleven. Our group of friends has an ice-cream container hidden near school with cigarettes in it stolen from our parents. The only brand I remember is Topaz. I don't remember smoking them, just the ice-cream container itself, with its four or five half-full packets. Once I start high school, my sister is smoking, so I start too. It gives me something to do in those frightening times around the margins of the day, the times when you need to have friends and somewhere to go: at the train station, before school waiting for the bell to ring, during playtime and lunchtime. When you smoke, you always have somewhere to be.

How clearly I remember the *stuff* of that early smoking! The feel of the cellophane wrapper, the red line of the strip that you pulled off, the way the plastic would cling to your hand with static electricity. You could slide the plastic sleeve down and burn a neat hole in the bottom of it, then blow in smoke and gently puff the packet to make smoke rings. You might be a plastic-off person, or you might keep the plastic on, and stretch it out to squeeze your cigarette lighter into. Usually you removed the gold or silver foil, but there were some people who kept it in there, which gave their packet a rumpled appearance; it wasn't shiny like the foil on chocolates, but matte, slightly patterned or embossed. The first thing to do, of course, when you opened a packet was to take out your lucky cigarette and turn it up the wrong way. You smoked that one last. By then it was a little loose at the end with tobacco that had fallen out. If you didn't have a lighter, you might be using matches. The taste of the first drag of a cigarette lit with matches! Unpleasant but utterly distinctive, the sulphurous, faintly eggy taste of the match head, and the heat and harshness of the smoke that is part sulphur, part wood, part tobacco, catching at the top of the throat. Of course your matchbox would have a lucky match in it too. If you didn't have a light or it was really windy you'd have to ask for a *monkey fuck*.

The main place to smoke at our school was *down the pines*. The older, cool kids—one had a trench coat and one had taken pills and actually been a prostitute!— would sit on the edge of the driveway closest to school, their legs hanging over the steep grassed bank above the playing field. The younger ones would stand further down, among the pine trees, talking about what the best brands of cigarettes were, or doing the alphabet in burps after sculling a bottle of Coke. Knee-length Swanndris were a thing, plain khaki ones or red-and-black checked. I fancied boys who wore jean jackets with sheepskin collars. A packet of Pall Mall twenties was $1.79.

Maybe I'm out of touch with smoking today, but there seemed to be a huge number of brands of cigarettes then compared to now. The brand you smoked was a way of asserting your identity, in straightforward ways—girls smoked menthol—or in more oblique attempts at self-expression. You could smoke Peter Stuyvesant Mild and people would say *It's like smoking air.* Or you could smoke Camel, which surely no one actually liked, but was, like, extra smokery. The main brand at our school was Winfield Red, maybe because it came in twenty-fives. I smoked them for a while, and I went through phases of Pall Mall, Peter Stuyvesant Blue, Stirling Menthol. Dunhill, either red or blue, was popular both with girls and with boys who were what I would now call *gay* but then, in third form, I would maybe have identified as *doing drama.* There were a number of novelty brands which people would try out but rarely stick with. At one point my sister smoked Cameo, which had a white satin finish to the filter. Then there was More, which was longer and thinner than a normal cigarette, more like a straw, and the cigarette paper was dark brown. They came in a soft packet which, given how delicate they were, was high risk. Fleur came in a floral packet and had orange and yellow flowers instead of words printed at its base.

In one of my favourite childhood books there was a scene in the Easter Bunny's palace, where all the Easter eggs of the world are stored. I got the same sense of incredible, almost infinite riches from the sight in a dairy of all of those brands of cigarettes, the different coloured, neatly wrapped, shining little boxes ranged above your head in racks, and how the shopkeeper would draw a packet out, and the dozens of packets above would move down to fill the space. I can feel myself asking for *a packet of Benson and Hedges and a box of matches*, something about the phrase itself having a mystical power even now as I say it aloud, maybe because there was a frisson, a screwing up of courage, an element of performance, knowing that you weren't old enough to be buying cigarettes. Though I don't remember ever being turned down.

The best thing about smoking was that you were never alone. Even when you were alone, if you went down the pines and there was no one there you knew, no one to talk to, you weren't *alone* alone, like you would have been if you'd been sitting on a bench somewhere. You had a reason to be where you were, and you had something to do, with your hands and your mouth and your eyes. And then the bell would go, and you'd gut drag the last bit, and walk back with the pine trees above you, past the incinerator, past the canteen, past the netball courts and back to class, reeking of smoke which you couldn't smell yourself, but which was in its own way a protective shield, because to be a rule-breaker was, in some way, to belong.

At home, Dad's Benson and Hedges were ever-present. Their gold packets were purchased in cartons of ten: Dad would rip the paper off a carton in what seemed to me such a gesture of plenty, and he'd keep the packets lined up on top of the fridge, above the mouse cage. He has notoriously awful handwriting, and he would often make notes on the back of his cigarette packet, the biro as much engraving as writing on the gold-foiled surface, rendering some esoteric scratchings like an archaeological treasure.

He had a number of Ronson lighters, which were refuelled with gas from a canister. One had a curved wooden base, the kind of lighter you'd keep on a table top. The one he carried most often was silver, streamlined like the fin of a 1950s car. You lit it by pushing down the top, and there was a wheel to adjust the height of the flame. It was the kind of lighter that was hard for kids to use. Dad would light it deftly with a flick of the wrist, and the sound it made I can hear now, like a piece of the machinery of my childhood. After 1979, when Mum and Dad went to Europe, he had his Concorde lighter. They brought back very little from that three-month trip: a black-and-white photo of boats at Marseille, an Egyptian print on papyrus, and their Concorde souvenirs: a navy blue towel embroidered with the Concorde 'C', and Dad's Concorde lighter, silver, faceted all over as if it had been hammered. It had an electronic spark which you could hear going *tick tick tick* if the lighter was low on gas and failing to catch. I don't recall ever seeing Dad use a plastic lighter. His silver lighter was one of those things that signified what an adult man would have: a silver lighter, and a leather jacket lined with paisley, and

47

of course an adult man would have moccasins, brown with a patch of cow skin at the front, a good pair for wearing around the house, and an older paint-spattered pair if you were doing jobs in the garage.

It seems strange, given how much smoking went on in our house, but I'm struggling to remember any ashtrays. I do remember the one at Dad's office though: cast metal set with coloured pebbles of glass. It was mainly ornamental—the one that Dad used was a large glass one, piled high with cigarette butts. While I waited for him to get off the phone, I'd look at the wall hanging, which was wool, with long skinny pennant-shaped points at the bottom, in tones of brown and yellow. Attached to it were little decorations—some were like pom poms, some like half-made pompoms, flat doughnuts of wool, including one gold one which I always liked to stick my finger into. If you have not lived through the Seventies and Eighties, it is hard to comprehend just how popular woollen wall hangings were as a form of corporate décor. Dad would be tipped right back in his chair, feet on his desk, his legs crossed at the ankles, talking and sometimes laughing with a loud *ha!* In his long fingers would be a cigarette, held vertically as it burned down to stop the ash from falling.

I'm not sure when I started rolling my own, but certainly by the time I was at university I was a dedicated rollie smoker. I carried my tobacco, my papers, my filters, and a lighter in a purple suede pouch. Rollies had advantages and disadvantages versus tailormades. On the downside, it was hard to roll a cigarette in the wind, or if you were really drunk. And little bits of tobacco would get everywhere—I still sometimes open an old book and find a thread of tobacco in it. But there were some great things about rolling your own. It gave an extra activity and ritual to smoking. It was an outlet for proficiency, something that you could do with studied ease, the filter pursed between your lips, or held in the V of your smallest fingers. And rolling your own defined you as a real smoker, not the social smoker for whom I felt only contempt—the kind of person who had never owned a lighter.

And I loved the tobacco itself: the smell of a fresh fifty-gram pouch of Port Royal, opening the pristine packet to the brown, orange and gold of the tobacco threads that, when fresh, would hold together and need to be fluffed apart. When you got down to the dregs, the tobacco would be dry and flaky—you'd roll a cigarette and half of it would fall out the end, the sticky tab of the packet would have lost its adhesion and have bits of tobacco all over it. Still, another advantage of rolling your own was that you never ran out of cigarettes—there was always a supply of old, nearly empty packets lying around with a few scraps of tobacco in the corners. And rollies, unlike tailormades, would go out if you left them in the ashtray, a particular advantage if you were a heavy dope smoker. It was not uncommon for me to roll a cigarette, take a puff, and go to put it down in the ashtray, then realise there was already an almost-full cigarette there which had gone out—or even two or three—next to a joint that had also gone out.

When you smoke, you spend a lot of time in strange places. As kids, we smoked in toilets, on train platforms, under the deck round the back of the hairdressers. When I got a bit older you could still smoke in lots of public places—even on planes. In coffee lounges you'd look for the *smoking section*, which seems such a strange phenomenon now. But eventually you couldn't smoke in offices, in malls, even in pubs. So you became someone who spends a lot of time in doorways, in the entrances of carparks, in places out the back of places. I sometimes think about that when I'm in a strange city, and I notice one of those leftover parts of the world—the back of a row of shops I saw in Fiji, with a man in his chef's whites standing outside smoking, or the dried-up outdoor garden of a university on the edge of Berlin, just a couple of benches set in a small concrete triangle between the buildings, with a tin to use as an ashtray. I think of how much of some people's lives will have been spent there, how much emotional weight these places will have, when the people who used them remember a life-changing conversation, or just standing there on a cold day, balancing a mug of coffee while they lit a cigarette against the wind.

As a smoker you forge unlikely alliances. One of my

first jobs was adjacent to the offices of Compass Shipping. It was a tiny company, just three people worked there, and they all smoked. After a while, instead of having my cigarette breaks outside on my own, I'd go next door to Compass Shipping and have my cigarette with Graeme. Graeme was in his fifties, with teenage twin daughters and a wife he was very much in love with. For some reason I always pictured her as looking like Carla on *Cheers*. There was a bit of a *Cheers* vibe to the whole thing really, sitting across the desk from Graeme in his small office while he talked about *certificates of lading* and other such nautical matters, the logo of P&O on the wall behind him on a wooden shield. It was a classic example of a smoker's friendship: those almost random connections you made, always having a reason to be in the same place at the same time, and always having a reason to leave—the cigarette like a steady fuse, burning down the time of your encounter to its natural ending.

Pretty much as soon as I started smoking, even as a girl of thirteen or fourteen, I tried to give up. But from my early twenties I began seriously attempting to stop smoking. I don't know how many times I stopped and started—dozens? Even a hundred? I had various techniques. I got rid of all my ashtrays, all my old packets of tobacco. I bought an ounce of cabbage—low quality, low strength marijuana—so I could smoke that instead. I told friends and family that I was stopping. Or I told no one, I just promised myself, throwing away my cigarettes

51

before bed, breaking them into pieces or soaking my tobacco in water. The next day, smoking would be constantly on my mind. The hardest thing would be getting home—if I could reach the front door, I could probably get through the night. But instead I might find myself at the dairy buying a ten-pack of Pall Mall—the thin, broad packet, a red tablet of failure and denial. The sense of inevitability, of self-contempt, relief, disgust—it became such a potent, recognisable mix, a dull, empty sensation of déjà vu.

I said affirmations—*I don't need this smokescreen any more*—and I read books—*By the time you finish this book you will have stopped smoking.* In one technique, I smoked ten a day for ten days, then five a day for five days. I wasn't allowed to do anything else when I smoked—not read or watch TV or listen to the radio. In the last days I could only smoke outside. And it worked! The technique worked. I stopped smoking for months, even for years. And then I'd have a night out, I'd be horribly drunk and I'd find myself in a brightly lit convenience store on Courtenay Place asking for *a packet of Benson and Hedges and a box of matches* and I'd light up, drawing the smoke into my mouth with the vacuum created by moving my tongue and cheeks and palate, then inhaling it into the lungs, that feeling as it crosses some point in the throat, that split second when it catches.

There wasn't anything special about the time when I finally did stop smoking, or maybe I should say, the last time I stopped. I just finished off my pouch of tobacco and threw out my last remaining ashtray, like I'd done so many times before.

There's a Billy Collins poem, 'The Best Cigarette', where he remembers his favourite moments of smoking. For me there's no contest: the best cigarette was the one you smoked after, or during, smoking a joint. The extra catch on your throat as it went down, the absolute *rightness* of that feeling, the sense of plenty, that everything you could want was right there, burning at your fingertips. But I can think of so many of the worst cigarettes: the first tailormade you smoke after a long spell of giving up, the taste of the match head and the fast-burning chemicals and of cheating yourself, like you knew you would. The one you smoke outside a restaurant, or a cinema, that constant mini-exile with its humiliating excuses. The one you smoke out the window of your non-judgemental non-smoking boyfriend's flat, though you know it pollutes his kitchen with his fresh basil and one really good knife and other evidence of grown-up wholesomeness. And the cigarette you smoke late at night, when you should have been in bed hours ago, but you stay up, smoking, and your mouth is like a cave, like a cavern, it feels burned and cauterised like it's made of bone.

Over decades of stopping and starting, I have thought a lot about the meaning of smoking. At first it's imitation, then rebellion. Then it becomes an identity, a social cover, something to be and something to hide behind. It's an emotional buffer, a smoke screen, something that gets between you and the world. Particularly as it became less socially acceptable, it was a means of escape, a reason to leave almost anywhere. I now view smoking almost as a philosophical activity, as a system for creating purpose. It is something you are always looking forward to at some level, either with positive anticipation, or with anxiety. It creates its own momentum. The precise opposite of living in the present, it is about living just ahead of where you are now, living in the time when you are having your next cigarette, or, perhaps more accurately, when you are no longer *not* having it. And, even if you have a cigarette already lit and half-smoked, you can be overtaken by the desire for a cigarette, because the desire is really not for the thing itself, it's for wanting something—and getting it.

I had wanted so many things. I wanted to be beautiful, like my sister. I wanted to look like a girl not a boy, and have breasts. I wanted to be touched, to be liked by the boys I liked, but they always liked someone different, someone prettier and shyer and shorter. I wanted to be good at things, to be brilliant, but I also wanted to be the rebellious, different one, the daredevil, the ringleader. And I wanted to be able to get things without anyone knowing I was trying—it needed to seem effortless. So smoking was a perfect engine of desire and fulfilment. Twenty times a day you wanted something, and you got it.

54

In my early twenties, a woman I worked with told me that she'd stopped smoking fifteen years before, back in South Africa, but that she still dreamed about it all the time. She was a brittle, sometimes difficult woman, and it seemed an unhelpful comment, given she knew I was trying to stop. But once I gave up, I started to have smoking dreams too. They'd follow a familiar pattern: some confused activity at the start, complications with a packet or a lighter, some long-forgotten doorway I was trying to get in or out of, or an odd half-remembered brand of cigarettes with words on the packet I couldn't read. And then, I'd be smoking, I'd see it in my hand, feel it in my throat, and while I was still in the dream I'd realise with horror—*I've started smoking again!* And the sensation was so familiar, not so much a sinking feeling, more a dull, dawning reality, an unsurprised disgust at myself, as if some piece of an awful puzzle had finally fallen into place, a feeling of *I should have known I'd end up back here.* The wash of relief, when I woke from those dreams, was radiant.

That ain't just friendship that's Beam

For a while in the Eighties there was a beer can that featured a scenic photograph of New Zealand: a snow-capped mountain, bush, maybe even a lake, in greens and blues like a faded postcard or a picture off a calendar. I stole one from the wash house once, where Dad must have had a box of them, and drank it with my friend in the bushes of the church before school, intermediate, we were probably eleven. And when I say we drank it, I mean we pretended we were drinking it, that we were getting drunk at eight in the morning, but we were actually pouring it out onto the ground while the other one wasn't looking. I remember playing in those same bushes with my friends after school, doing 'Indies' which is when you pretend to be Indiana Jones by jumping off things in an adventurous manner.

Early teenage drinking. I'm falling out of a flax bush with a friend from school that I have a big crush on. I hope we're going to kiss but we don't. I'm walking down the middle of a suburban street, singing 'Rocky Raccoon' at the top of my voice. I'm at a party at my neighbour's house, her big sister's party, who is at university, and I'm drinking gin and talking to a guy with big tortoiseshell Eighties glasses—is he wearing some kind of tweedy jacket or does my mind add that in? I'm in the third form, and I'm wearing borrowed white high heels that I got from god knows where, and then I'm telling my friend later, how I said to him *if you try anything I'm going to put this heel right through your foot*. I can't imagine I said that, or that he tried anything, and my friend surely knows it never happened too, but she plays along. We are collaborators in a rich fantasy life.

One thing I knew about being drunk was that when you were drunk you did stupid things, outrageous things, things you wouldn't do otherwise. And I knew that boys would get you drunk so they could do sex stuff with you, so by being drunk or pretending to be drunk you could go with a boy and not have to admit you wanted to, if he wasn't cool, or spunky, or you didn't really know him, or maybe he was with someone else, was way older than you, or off limits in some other way. But when you were *pissed*, well, who knows what you might do? And you probably wouldn't even remember it afterwards, so people would be telling you what had happened, what you'd done, or what had been done to you, you'd be finding hickeys on your neck, and you'd be able to be shocked, like it had been someone else all along. Before I had ever been drunk I knew all that, that being drunk would let you be someone different.

At another party at their house, I'm properly drunk this time, in the spa pool with all my clothes on, my tartan woollen miniskirt from Top Shop in London, and my woollen tights, and I think that's the same party where I have sex for the first time, where I *lose my virginity* in my friend's sister's bed which is only three-quarter length so my feet hang off the end. It's with my best friend's boyfriend. I don't remember much, just how his penis seemed to veer off to the side, rather than be straight, which was a neutral surprise. I'm fourteen, which I feel good about, because to lose your virginity at fourteen is pretty out there, but it's not really shockingly early in a tragic way, like it would be to lose your virginity at thirteen, like in *Puberty Blues*. In the morning my friend and I go to Family Planning together to get the morning-after pill. We laugh about what the doctor must think when we give our addresses: number twelve and number eight of the same street.

My first drinking injury happens in 1987. Mum is away overnight at her French camp, Dad has moved out, so my sister and I have the house to ourselves. Being a younger sister means hanging out with an older crowd. My sister's friends have cars, and can buy their own alcohol from a bottle store, or maybe they get it from their older siblings. We're all somewhere drinking Jim Beam and Southern Comfort, and then we're in cars, heading into the city, to a place that's just opened recently, and a phenomenon that's only just started—we're going to a *café*, to Clowns Café, in Stout Street by the bus depot. There's four yellow-doored phoneboxes at that bus stop and you always stop and press button B in all of them, in case there's money that hasn't been refunded.

Clowns Café is underground, that's all I can tell you about it. It's underground, and we're sitting around a corner table or a booth, and there's stainless-steel teapots in front of us because this is well before espresso, and I'm wearing khaki trousers and a tuxedo shirt with tails, and I throw up, a very liquid vomit made up mostly of Jim Beam, and it spreads and flows instantly over the table, and everyone's shrieking and scrambling to push their chairs back. Then I'm on the street, I've taken my trousers off so I'm just in my undies and a shirt, but a part of me feels OK about that, because it's a long shirt, a shirt with tails. Then we're back at home, in the games room under our double garage. No doubt there's music blaring on the tape deck, probably the Eagles' greatest hits. I'm standing in the doorway to the outside, getting some fresh air. It's a stormy, southerly night, and a wind gust slams the door shut, from fully open to fully shut, like the cover of a book. My left index finger is at the exact point on the doorframe where the lock connects, and as it shuts it hits the fingertip with huge force, and there's blood, but *I'm fine* I'm telling everyone, I can't really feel a thing, and someone puts a Band-Aid on it, and on we go until, at some point we hear a car pull into the garage above us. Mum's French Camp has been cancelled.

The next morning there's patches of blood on the sheet, on my pillow, on the wall. The pain of my finger is awful, absolutely hideous—all those nerve endings—and it's throbbing constantly in time with my pulse. I need to go to the hospital, to A&E, but Mum won't take me, she says she'll drop me at the train station when she goes to work and I can make my way from there. The atmosphere in the car is tense, then I'm on the bus, and I have to hold the finger up above my heart, otherwise the throbbing is unbearable, so I look like someone timidly raising their hand for attention.

They give me four injections of local anaesthetic around the base of the finger, and explain that the lock of the door hit with such force it broke the nail in two, and the bottom half of the fingernail has been pushed under the skin down to where the knuckle is and they need to go in and get it. The nail might grow back they say, or maybe not, if the nail bed has been too badly damaged. It's extremely painful, and I'm also horribly hungover, but part of me can already tell that this will be a great story, because I know that's what happens when you get drunk: you pile into cars and drive too fast, you throw up, you end up without your trousers, you hurt yourself and you get in trouble and all of these make great stories.

It truly is a binge-drinking *culture* with its language and rituals and mythologising. Our group of friends has an elaborate handshake for a while, with different clasps and pinkie finger–holding and who knows what, and as you do it you chant in unison *That! Ain't! Just! Friendship! That's! Beam!* I honestly don't know who we thought we were.

Our teenage drinking took place mainly outdoors, at the Waru Street bus stop (Wuru Street bar stop), or at Khandallah Park, in the dappled shadow of trees, black hillsides against the lighter, orange–black sky, the giddy mania that is partly drink, partly the cold night air making your eyes and nose run, partly the running, from noises and people and adults, and the laughing, the showy hilarity as we convince ourselves how drunk we are, how crazy. *Squat drop drip dry fart burp hoik* is one of the sayings we have, my sister and I and our next-door neighbour, because we are always pissing outside, squatting together in the cold. One night our gay friend gets us 'rush'—amyl nitrate—and we get into that for a while, the thirty seconds of roller-coaster thrill, and then the instant, head-throbbing comedown. Even the first time I tried it, I could tell how horrible it was, but there we are, on the footpath along Burma Road, grabbing at the bottle and spilling it on our hands, feeling the coolness as it evaporates off in an instant. And you can bet we would have kept going until it was all gone.

I'm at home one time, pretending to be sick off

school. My sister isn't there but her boyfriend and his friend come round, and we get drunk together. We're drinking Chardon, which everyone used to scrape the C off the label of, or just cover it with their finger. And then I'm having sex with my sister's boyfriend, at least I think I am, yes I am, because I remember thinking that his dick is a lot bigger than I expect it to be, not longer but thicker, and his friend is there, watching I assume, and at some point they're fucking me with the Chardon bottle, and I look at it later and see that there's some kind of white residue around the neck of the bottle and feel embarrassed, hope they won't notice. And I suppose it's a sexual assault, I mean it *is* a sexual assault, because I'm obviously in no fit state to consent, but what I remember is that I wanted it to happen, I wanted to do it, because I wanted the sexual attention, and I wanted to be up for anything, to amaze others with just how far I was prepared to go. That had always been my thing, from a three-year-old with Christmas blow-outs stuck up my nostrils, to a ten-year-old waving from the tallest climbing pole—*Look at me, look at what I will do.*

That night I write in my diary *I think I screwed Jason* with about twenty exclamation marks, and on some level I'm hoping my sister will read it and find out but she doesn't. It's only years later, in my twenties, that I tell her about it. And then I tell her about it again in my thirties, when I find the diary again, and then in my forties, when I find it again, because I'm reading from it at Bad Diaries

Salon. And each time she says *Yeah I know, you told me about it before.* I still don't know how she feels about it. Probably not very much, like I don't. It's just another neutral half-memory of teenagehood.

From thirteen I was able to get into pubs. There was no ID needed in those days, you just had to look old enough, and I was tall, and had a low voice, and with a borrowed bra stuffed with tissues, wearing clothes from Mum's wardrobe, I could get into the 1860 on Lambton Quay, or the Oaks on Dixon Street. It was always touch-and-go of course, you'd be nervous the whole time, smoking at a table and letting other people buy your Bacardi and Coke. One night we were walking back to the train station past Midland Park. It had a waterfall fountain, like a big urinal, and someone had put detergent in it so there were banks of bubbles built up and blowing down the street. We stopped to play with the foam for a while. One night we got talking to some guys, we asked them to guess how old we were, and they guessed I was twenty-four, and when I said you're ten years off one of them said *You're not thirty-four!* I used to show off that I could go to the pub, and then catch the train home as a half.

Pubs closed at ten, which meant you could catch the eleven-oh-four, with time to stop at the pie cart for a punnet of chips soaked in malt vinegar. It was the only place at that time of night that you could buy cigarettes, not the full range, just the basics: Rothmans, Pall Mall,

Benson and Hedges, Dunhill. The whole way home we'd be telling stories of what had happened that night, embellishing them, to become part of our shared store of anecdotes. And then we'd go back to our neighbour's house, because you could get into her room by an outside door. Her parents thought she was staying at our place, and our parents thought we were staying at hers, so no one knew that we'd arrived home near midnight, with our blue-and-pink eyeshadow and middle-aged clothes, pantyhose and pumps, which we'd sneak back into our mothers' wardrobes the next day.

By the time I could drink legally, I'd become such a pothead that I only drank at home, or places where I could get stoned at the same time. Cuba Cuba had an outside area with a fire, and I used to go there and drink pints of cider and smoke joints. I was at university but the friends I went with weren't university friends—one was a girl I knew a little from school who I'd met again at a holiday job, one was my old downstairs flatmate Mark, who'd lived with my sister for a while and now was single again, another was an ex-workmate, a guy in his late thirties who I used to play Scrabble with. I remember Mark saying to me once that he envied the friends on *Friends*, how they had that close group to hang out with. *But what about us guys*, I said, *we're a group of friends that hangs out together? Not like that*, he said, *we're just a group of sad lonely people with no one else to hang out with*. It was true, but I was startled to hear him say it out loud, and also shocked that he'd mention *Friends* in such an unironic light, Mark who was cynical about everything. By the end of a night at Cuba Cuba, I'd be so drunk I could hardly speak, and I'd get into a taxi and summon up all the clarity I could to say my address once, *one-four-five Kelburn Parade*. Then I'd sit in silence for the journey, trying desperately to keep my head upright, and then give the driver money, maybe not wait for the change, just stagger out of the cab, fumble the door unlocked, and into bed. I always felt I wouldn't be able to say my address twice.

I rarely went out to restaurants, but we did get kicked out of Aro Café one time at a birthday dinner for my flatmate. We came home and kept the party going, the phone rang and rang, and finally our elderly neighbour came to the door in her quilted dressing gown, and none of us would answer it, we ran screaming into our bedrooms. The next morning I was sick for the first time ever the morning after—I'd been sick many times while drunk, but never the next day. I remember seeing myself in the bathroom mirror as I threw up in the sink, the white of my eyes bright red with the irises blue against them, and the yellow bile, remember noticing the primary colours. Come to think of it, I'd been sick the night before too, thrown up in my hair once I'd gone to bed. I'd had Cajun blackened fish for dinner—how very Nineties.

In my early thirties I got my first management job,

kind of by accident. Our work had a culture of epic Friday drinks. Like at every workplace, it relied on one stalwart organiser and she'd be there late Friday afternoon, cutting up frozen sausage rolls, and then the tea room would fill up, and before you knew it you'd be shouting to be heard, red-faced and sweating with the air con turned off, and then the crowd would thin out, only the real drinkers would be left, people would be dancing, standing on tables, catching the lift downstairs to go out for a cigarette, and I'd be in the work toilets, rushing to have a piss and get back to the action, seeing myself flushed and wild-eyed in the mirror. Around nine we'd bail out of work and walk up to Courtenay Place, and of course on the way I'd stop and buy tobacco: thirty grams of Port Royal, a packet of yellow Zig-Zags, a packet of slim filters and a lighter. It always felt obvious to me when I did this that I was falling off the wagon, because no regular smoker buys all those things at once. I'd know that I was doing something I'd regret but I was drunk! So drunk! I sometimes wondered if I drank so much in order to smoke, to give myself that excuse.

We'd drink at Mirror bar and Electric Avenue and Kitty O'Shea's. A friend got turned away there one night for being intoxicated. *Of course I'm intoxicated*, he told the bouncer, *this is Kitty O'Shea's*. We'd end up in places where I had no idea where I was and I'd be going to the bar and preparing myself to enter my PIN, to speak without slurring, control my lazy eye which would be all over the place once I was a few drinks in. And eventually, at one or two or three in the morning, I'd bail, an Irish goodbye, just leave, not say anything to anyone, didn't want to be a party pooper. I'd bought my house in Mount Cook by then so I'd walk home up Taranaki Street, sometimes able to keep a fairly straight line, sometimes staggering from lamppost to lamppost, straightening up when I heard a car coming behind me. I wasn't oblivious to how risky it was—even in my drunken state I tried to keep out of the shadows, away from driveways or the bushes—but sometimes I'd be so drunk it was all I could do to keep upright, stopping to lean against a wall, a rubbish bin, just dragging one heavy leg in front of the other. I'd keep an eye out for safe-seeming people I could walk near to. One night it was the Sevens, and I fell in with a group of Biblical prophets for a while. Further on, alone again, I saw another group across the road, eating fish and chips from a white paper packet. *Hey flamingos,* I called out, *can I have a chip?* And all of this was fine, it was normal, on Monday at work we'd compare notes, what time we'd got home, how we'd looked at our EFTPOS to see where we'd been, the parts of the night we did and didn't remember.

Sometimes there'd be midweek benders too, when we had some kind of work function and carried on from there. I remember rolling out of the Port Nick Yacht Club very worse for wear, ending up at an outside table on a freezing cold night, chain-smoking and drinking into the small hours with a work friend, a clever guy, brilliant really, I'm sure we had a fascinating conversation with our slurred words and red-wine teeth, but of course I can't remember it. The next day I booked a long meeting into my diary at lunchtime, and went to my car in the parking building and slept, with the seat tipped back and a jacket over my face. As I woke up with the dry, tacky mouth of a daytime sleeper I thought, *Maybe my drinking is getting out of hand.*

Eventually I aged out of the Courtenay Place drinking. I was a secret smoker, and pot smoker, and I became a secret drinker too. I made a new friend. He was the only person I knew who smoked weed because I'd cut myself off from my old world. He'd come round to my place on a Friday, and I'd have beers in the fridge for me, and bottles of wine for him, and he'd bring the weed, and we'd sit and get stoned and talk for hours, and we'd sing and dance, to Fleetwood Mac or Janis Ian's 'Fly Too High', shouting in each other's faces over the stereo, and one time the neighbour came over and put her head through the sash window and said *Please, I have to work tomorrow*, and we laughed later at how she was probably expecting a huge party, and found just the two of us. I never wanted him to leave but eventually he would, he'd walk back home, and in the morning I'd get up to look after my nephew who was a toddler then, I'd make him baked beans in a stripy bowl or a spotty bowl, and I'd walk him up and down the street in the stroller, and then put him to sleep on cushions on the floor. I told him the story of the three wise men, of Caspar, Melchior and Balthazar, and when I asked him later why they came to see Jesus he said *Because they saw the moon*. That was how I spent my hangovers, watching over this little boy, and it was beautiful.

I don't drink often now, have never been a glass of wine with dinner person, would rather have a cup of tea. But even in my forties I've had some *huge nights*, out dancing late with no memory of the Uber home, asked for a shot and a beer and been told I can have the beer but not the shot, nights when I've been sick the next day, when I've pissed on the floor at the end of the bed, family parties when I've tried to use Spotify but been too drunk to read the phone, asking my now-teenage nephew to play Neil Young's 'Old Man' and he says *I played that for you an hour ago*. And five minutes later I ask him again. And then again.

This wheel's
on fire

There's a feeling I never get now, haven't had for years, but I used to get it all the time. It's the feeling of waking up in the morning after you've been up late the night before, crying and screaming, locked in a fight that goes on for hours. You're crying so much that your eyes aren't just red, they're swollen, your nose is swollen, your face and throat is all blotchy, and you whip yourself into an ever-greater state of anger, of poisonous contempt, you say things you know are so unfair, deploy your powers of sarcasm, argument, cruelty. And then there's a breaking point, furniture gets smashed, a hole punched in the wall, maybe you're held by the throat, with someone shouting in your face. And after that it winds down. Eventually you go to bed. When you wake up in the morning your eyes are still swollen, and there's a strange feeling in your body, like poison has passed through it.

I spent ten years of my teens and twenties with an

on-again-off-again boyfriend, and we used to fight like that all the time. I remember our downstairs neighbour saying to me one time, *When I hear you guys fight, and I can hear things smashing and breaking, and I hear you screaming, when should I call the police?* And I didn't skip a beat, didn't think, *I wonder if that's a rhetorical question.* I just said, *I'll call out to you. If I ever call your name, go straight next door and call the cops.* He didn't have a phone.

The first time I saw Jimi is actually the first time he saw me. I know about it now because he told me at some point, some point when I was young enough to find it flattering, not creepy. He said, *I used to see you from the window walking up Holloway Road and think . . .* I can't remember what he said he thought, it would have been something about my arse. I would have been wearing skintight jeans—we didn't call them skinny jeans then—grey ones which I thought were so much more sophisticated than the black ones every other girl had, every other girl who hung around with the wrong crowd, or wanted to.

I would have been walking up Holloway Road to my friend Tony's house, right up the top. Had I rung in advance? Maybe, or maybe I just turned up, because Tony was always home. He was a solo dad, and he was forty-one, which seemed an almost surreal age for anyone to be who smoked dope and lived the way he did. Tony made forty-one seem cool, not old. He was handsome, and a bit camp, and he was kind—I always felt safe around Tony, he had a sly humour, and he would drive me home, at two or three or four in the morning. However late it was he would get in his car and drive me home to my mum's place in Thorndon.

I'd met Tony through my high-school boyfriend Craig. Craig had long hair and a jean jacket and an interest in Nazi memorabilia. His Dad was a plumber and Craig was good at making things. He made a hash pipe for me out of an empty tin of model airplane paint. The smell of hash was lovely, so sweet and fragrant, and it was nice smoking it from the pipe that my boyfriend had made for me. Craig was selling the hash at school, on a small scale, just to friends. And he was getting it from Tony.

The only distinct memory I have of my time with Craig was being in his room, doing sex stuff on his bed, which at that time meant kissing and hoping a guy would feel you up, but also needing to go through a theatre of resisting. You had to pretend you didn't want him to put his hand up your shirt and touch your breast, that you didn't want him to put his hand down your skintight jeans, even though when he did you were so wet you worried you'd just suddenly got your period. And you never reached down and put your hand on the crotch of his jeans to feel his teenage erection hard against the denim, but he might move your hand there and then it was OK to kind of grab it through the fabric and half hold it, half rub it. And while we were in there, his father

72

yelled out *You better keep that door open I know what you kids are up to in there.* I couldn't imagine my parents ever saying something like that. For my fifteenth birthday his mother bought me the *Alison Holst Kitchen Diary*, which had blank pages where you can write your own recipes, and I remember thinking *Wow, she really doesn't get who I am.* I still have the book though, and it does have recipes written into it.

My other memory is Craig coming to pick me up on his motorbike from Dad's place, the feeling of being a girl who gets picked up by her boyfriend on a motorbike and, with her over-large bobbly-feeling helmet head, puts her feet on the pegs and puts her arms around his small, skinny body, smelling the leather of his tight, dark brown jacket, and he's got that not-ready-to-shave unsightly teen boy moustache face, like he's a fan of Crosby, Stills, Nash and Young, which he is. It was a wonderful feeling, even if you knew he wasn't the proper motorbike-riding boyfriend, who would have been taller and handsomer and had a bigger bike, and even if you knew you weren't the proper motorbike-riding girlfriend, who would have been shorter and prettier, with boobs and no glasses. But there was still a sense of inhabiting the outlines of glamour which was exhilarating.

It was through Craig that I met Tony, going up there to Holloway Road on the back of his bike to score hash. Tony would come to the door and always open it with a smile. On one side of the hallway was a wallpaper mural of giant poppies, reflected in a full-height mirror wall on the other side. In the lounge, where I must have spent hundreds, thousands of hours, there was another wallpaper mural, an autumnal forest in shades of yellow and green. Everyone sat on the other side of the room, on a brown lounge suite, and there was a bottle wall next to that, made of wine bottles set in concrete so the light could shine through them, but I don't remember it doing that, because Holloway Road never got much sun, and the bottles had got dirty and had spider webs and leaves in them, and it all leaked a bit and didn't really hold together.

It could get so cold there at night, and I remember one time lying on the floor with Tony after drinking opium-poppy tea, and we put our legs up on the grey metal top of the heater and looked at the ceiling and chatted. It was the small hours of the morning, everyone who hung around the house had gone, the kids had gone to bed. Such a sense of quiet intimacy. It didn't seem strange to me that one of the people I was closest to, as a fifteen-year-old girl, was a forty-one-year-old drug dealer. And it never occurred to me that he was a father figure—that, with Dad having left Mum only a year before, I was seeking out this solo father, who was gentle, and funny and kind, and who was rich and powerful too, in a way, because in a world of druggies and people on the dole he had a house, and drove a Rover, and had the first carphone I ever saw, that anyone ever saw, its spiral cord coming up from between the front seats.

Tony's sons were seven and twelve when I met them. The younger one would go crazy, practising wrestling moves in front of a sofa full of pot-heads. The older one was pretty and over-groomed—with his collared shirts and gelled hair he affected a preppie air, the ultimate act of rebellion. The presence of the kids lent a wholesomeness to the place, a family feeling, even though they were clearly troubled, and by definition at risk, living in a house full of people, mainly men, in all sorts of states of life crisis. I liked kids, and I had a rescuer complex, and so I poured my energy into them, listening to their stories, making in-jokes, giving them the attention they craved. I had them up to the beach house one weekend, and we played on the beach and gathered firewood. I have a photograph of the youngest one carrying back a huge log over his shoulder—he was always full of manic energy. I knew these kids were deprived, their life was fucked up, and I was part of that, but I also thought I could be a respite from it. Even though I spent more time at Tony's than just about anyone, I knew I wasn't really part of that world, I was a tourist, with a bungee cord of privilege that would always snap me back to safety. I can see myself there in Tony's kitchen at one in the morning, with a Wettex thick with Jif, scrubbing off the ancient grease behind the deep fryer. It wasn't so different from the forts we built as children, with chicken-wire windows and curtains drawing-pinned above. Playing mum, playing house.

Lots of people would pass through Tony's place, stop in to buy hash and then stay to smoke it, maybe watch some WWF wrestling on TV with the kids, Hulk Hogan era, or just talk shit and listen to music, The Cowboy Junkies or something equally relaxed—Tony's was never a place for loud music. On one of those aimless afternoons I met Greg. I was still with my high-school boyfriend, but to my mind, there was no contest. Greg was a *man*, he was twenty-three I think, worked on the ferries earning what seemed like a fortune and spending it all on partying. He was heavily tattooed: dozens of skulls on one arm, with wolves howling at the moon around the elbow, and a topless woman on the other, to one side of her a bottle marked XXXX, to the other a wad of cash and a marijuana leaf, and written on the unfurling ribbon below her torso *Sailor's Dream*. When we were going out, I drew glasses on her with a biro, to make her look like me.

It was apparent to everyone that Greg had a crush on me. And I liked him too. He could be very funny, mostly because there was nowhere he wouldn't go, nothing he wouldn't say, to get a laugh. He told us about being in the roughest pub in New Plymouth and tongue-kissing his friend, who was the lead singer of a punk band, just to freak out the locals. He explained that he had *Bus Depot* tattooed on his bum cheek. At parties he'd walk around asking anyone if they knew where the nearest bus depot was, until everyone started asking each other, and finally someone asked him. Then he'd downtrou and show them. I don't know if it ever actually happened, but that was the story, and he did have the tattoo.

Greg was a terrible alcoholic, just awful, the kind who routinely drinks until they pass out. I remember being at the pub once when he lost consciousness in a booth, sitting straight up, conked out drooling with a beer still in his hand. I can see the string of saliva hanging, transparent, off his surprisingly sensual lower lip. I couldn't wake him up and had to climb over the back of the booth to get out. Greg was a stocky, brawny guy, and there was an undercurrent of menace in his drinking, of violence. Never towards me, I want to say, but when you have a partner who gets into violent rages and hurts people, even if you're not there, on some level it is still a threat. He would get upset at me over something, storm off, and then he'd tell me later that he'd punched someone on the street, or gotten into a fight with a taxi driver.

There was something self-consciously chivalrous about Greg, tied to the culture of seamanship. His dad had been a wharfie and his mum was a barmaid at the Thistle, where in those days all the seamen drank. It wasn't just that he would walk on the road side of the footpath, or open doors, or give you the last cigarette— although he did all that. It was a vintage sense of *how men behaved*, that you would always be free with your money and spend your last dollar on a drink for a friend. That you would acknowledge hospitality, honour your mother and shake hands with eye contact. His identity wavered between 1950s hard man with a heart of gold, and punk rock outrage machine with no boundaries. In the back of a taxi one day, he put his arm along the back of the seat, and the next time we went around a corner, I let myself lean into it. And that was the start of that.

The reaction to Greg from my mother wasn't quite what I thought it would be—what, if I'm honest, I hoped it would be. She didn't seem appalled by him at all, in fact she seemed to view him more with an indulgent pity, a sense that he was out of his depth with me, rather than the other way around. She used to joke about it with her friends, that I'd brought home this heavily tattooed sailor who had no idea what he'd gotten into, that was the tone as I remember it. Greg worked week on week off, and when he was ashore he would walk over to see me at Mum's house in Thorndon, across the rail yards from the ferry terminal. I'd be sitting in my shed in the courtyard of Mum's historic villa, an extension cord running from the house to power my heater and tape deck. I had a single divan bed in there, and a tea trolley I'd salvaged from a Burke's bin, and the walls were covered in pictures of the Beatles cut out from a book, and a handwritten poster of the cards of the tarot deck. And I'd be in there reading A.N. Wilson or Julian Barnes or true crime books with their yellow-edged pages, and Greg would arrive, I'd hear him unlatch the gate, and I'd put on a tape like Rickie Lee Jones and pinch my cheeks, maybe undo a button of my black muslin shirt, which smelled, like I did, of patchouli incense. And we'd get stoned, and have sex and lie on the divan, smoking. He would always light my cigarette first. And the sex wasn't good, it was terrible really, he'd be banging away for ages, while I was loudly faking it—I don't think I'd ever had an orgasm. But I was happy to be doing it, something I wasn't supposed to be doing, something that meant I was feminine, and attractive and wanted, and I was getting turned on along the way, even by accident, and then there was the lying around afterwards, out of reach of the ashtray, holding our cigarettes as vertical as possible until Greg would hold out a cupped hand for me to tip my ash into.

Because of his shifts on the ferry, Greg was at sea for seven or ten days at a time, so I was still up at Tony's a lot on my own. A guy called Jimi, who lived down the road, became a regular visitor. He was tall, lean and goodlooking, with green eyes and brown hair in a short mullet. I'm not sure in what order I became aware of key facts about him, but he was twenty-eight, a dope-grower, a pig-hunter with a pack of dogs. He was involved with Tony's ex, who was a junkie. And he was volatile—I knew that from the start, that he had a temper. He loved to talk, hadn't had much education but was a bright guy, liked to read about Celtic mythology, ley lines, the Vikings. In Tony's lounge, with a bunch of strays drinking coffee from Arcoroc mugs, he held forth, held court, talking on and on, and everyone listened, because he had pot. He always had incredible pot which he'd grown himself, and he'd roll enormous joints, engineered with excruciating precision, and while he rolled them he had a captive audience. I never thought of it at the time, just thought how fucking annoying it was that he took so long to roll a joint, but it's sad to think now how much he needed that audience. He must have known, on some level, that he was buying his place in the circle, that if he hadn't had pot people would have told him long ago to shut up, or just got up and left, but we all waited, the teenage school kid, the forty-something acid burn-out, whoever had washed up at Tony's on a weekday afternoon.

I have always been a talker, and I'm sure it annoyed a lot of people, but it would have been part of the attraction for Jimi. He envied my education, and he loved to talk about ideas, to learn and use obscure words, loved to play Scrabble. And then there was the physical attraction. I was seventeen, tall and slim with my long curly hair dyed red or sometimes black. Because I had glasses, and small tits, I never considered myself attractive, but of course I was beautiful, the way a young woman is, in my skintight jeans, leather waistcoat and love beads—it was 1989 but dressed for 1969.

Even before we got together, I knew that Jimi wouldn't

treat me well. He was arrogant and high-handed, had other women he was involved with. He wouldn't be *cunt struck* like Greg. But he had unlimited supplies of pot, and I respected him. Greg was a bit of a joke, especially to himself. His crazy behaviour, his ridiculous drinking— even the way he worshipped me was a bit pathetic. I was impressed by Jimi. He was driven, ambitious, was good at something. He was someone who knew gang members, murderers, and they rated him, by his own account. How much of this was real, how much his self-mythologising, how much my own projection I don't know, but that was how I saw him: handsome, smart and dangerous. A force to be reckoned with.

Now I'm standing at the doorway of our relationship, I feel exhausted. I try to remember some good times, some ordinary times. Laughing at him drying his undies in the oven. Chasing down a weka that stole our pot while we slept in the car. Being in a bath when an earthquake happened, the water sloshing between us. Getting an electric shock from the leak in his waterbed. Eating plums on the roof of the car, picked from a roadside rest stop. Dancing in my flatmate's room while he watched through the window. Singing at full volume in the wind and him saying *You can really sing*. And there was the sex, of course. I was still faking it which wasn't helping anyone, but Jimi found me beautiful. I had all sorts of lingerie that I'd stolen from a lingerie sale I worked at. It was the first time I'd ever had lacy bras and pants, suspenders and stockings, and there was a theatre to it, I played the role of a sexy woman and it felt good.

I don't think I ever perceived him as *committing domestic violence*. I knew what that was of course, I was a feminist, I'd seen the graffiti *If he beats you, leave.* I think that, because he never hit me, I thought it didn't count. And also because I knew what I was like when we were fighting, how enraged I would get, that I would say things to damage him, never take a step back, just keep escalating and escalating, or I'd use my superpower, cultivated since childhood, of appearing not to care, seeming unaffected in the face of his building hysteria. So when he would finally break, and he would do something like take the vacuum cleaner pipe and hit himself in the head with it, the hollow plastic resounding with an almost musical note, or tip a bucket of water over me, or punch a hole in the wall by my head, or grab me by the throat, when he did those things there was a part of me that didn't blame him, that knew he'd been goaded into it, understood he was acting out of desperation, like an injured animal, just wanting to show how upset he was, to break through my obliviousness, my calm disdain.

And I would always fight right up to the brink, never give in, never give a millimetre, never say sorry or back down—until he got violent. And then I would, immediately. I would just concede, and I'd be ducking my head and holding my hands up in front of my face to ward him off, like a woman in a movie. And it's because of those times that I always know, when I'm reading about people enduring torture or defying the threat of violence, I know I wouldn't do that. Because even when I'd be dripping with anger and condescension, knowing I was right, when he pulled back his hand and formed a fist, I gave in, in a heartbeat.

We fought constantly, everyone around us knew that: my flatmates, my sister who lived with us for a while, the neighbours. They probably heard things breaking—I remember him throwing a plate of food at the wall in my bedsit, and the Arcoroc plate broke, and bits of the smoked glass and baked beans were stuck for a long moment to the wall. But I don't remember him ever threatening me in front of anyone, ever raising a hand to me. Maybe that was another reason I accepted it, because it was happening where other people couldn't see. I don't remember telling anyone about it, but maybe I did tell them, or maybe they had a pretty good idea. In the world we were living in, or dabbling in, there was violence, there were crimes committed, there were dangerous situations, and compromises made.

I was still living at home with Mum when I got arrested for the first time. Jimi and Jimi's best friend and I were in the shed getting stoned. It was late, close to midnight, a quiet night sitting around in our socks. The shed was tiny, just room for a single bed and an armchair. As well as dope smoke and cigarette smoke, the air would have been grey with incense. There might have

83

been a split-second warning, a sound or a shape outside the window, and then the door flew open, inward, and two or three men burst in to the tiny space. They were wide-eyed and breathless, and one of them had a gun, a pistol, that he was pointing all around. And they shouted something like *Police police nobody move!* My first thought was, this isn't the police—they weren't in uniform, and they looked panicked, and they had a gun. I was terrified, thinking we were being ripped off, my mind scrambling through worst case scenarios.

Once I realised it actually was the police, I was so relieved I was almost giddy. I kept saying to them, *you scared the hell out of me coming in that way!* Now my fear moved in a different direction—that the noise would wake my mother, asleep upstairs. They had heard that Jimi had a crossbow, which he did, and that was why they had come with guns, because they were arresting him on an assault charge and believed he was armed and dangerous. A bunch of Jimi's stuff was upstairs in the spare room, and I pleaded with the cops to be quiet, that I would sneak up and get the crossbow without waking Mum. They let me go upstairs and quietly bring it down. At some point they saw a tin of heads on the tea trolley in the shed. It was an old, hinged tobacco tin, and there was probably the equivalent of a hundred-buck bag in there, maybe a quarter or a fifth of an ounce. They asked whose it was and I said *It's mine*, because it was, and because, while all this was happening and my heart was still racing, another part of me was already in the future, imagining this as a story we'd be telling, and in that story I wasn't going to narc, or let a friend go down for something that was mine. They searched Jimi's car and found a jar of seeds and a roll of chicken wire, and that was it. We put our shoes on and they took us in to the station.

The cop who interviewed me was young and handsome, with a leather jacket. I don't remember the interview well, just that there was an offer to let me off if I turned on Jimi, and also the information that he was being charged with *assault on a female* for choking his ex. I don't remember what I thought about this, probably that she was crazy, and volatile and violent herself, an inveterate liar, and that whatever had happened it wouldn't have been what she said it was, and whatever it had been, it wasn't the kind of thing that could happen to me. Even though it had happened to me.

The part I remember most clearly was being fingerprinted. The cop, in uniform, stood close beside me, like a partner in a folk dance. He took my hand and rolled each finger over the ink pad, then we took a step forward together, and he rolled it onto the paper, within the designated square. We stepped back and forth together for the four fingers, and then the extra awkwardness of the thumb. It was like a doctor putting a stethoscope on your back, or a hairdresser tipping your head to the side: someone else taking charge of your body with practised authority, intimate yet impersonal.

I got diversion which meant I did drug counselling and community service, and didn't get a criminal conviction. In the lead-up to Jimi's court case I came to an understanding of what had happened, based, of course, on what he told me. He and his ex had got into a fight, and Jimi had waved around his ornamental sword from Bali, which wasn't sharp, and had a blade so flimsy you could bend it with your hand. She had hit him on the head with a hammer causing a big lump, and he had held her up against the wall by the throat. All this had happened at Tony's house. And she'd pressed charges, as far as Jimi was concerned, out of spite, with the bruises on her throat as evidence. I never questioned his version of events, except I knew that him waving a sword around would be terrifying, even if you thought or even "knew" he wasn't going to do anything with it.

There was a witness: Tony's fourteen-year-old son had seen it happen, or he said he had. And I suppose every story, every court case, is like this, but it was complicated, because Tony's son had a schoolboy crush on me and because of that he hated Jimi. It was a surreal feeling to find myself in the Wellington District Court, part of this soap opera, with the victim this crazy junkie, the defendant my violent boyfriend, and the lead witness a fourteen-year-old boy dressed like a trainee stockbroker. It was an afternoon hearing, with sun pouring in through the windows, and people spoke so fast the stenographer couldn't keep up and at one point she burst into tears and the judge had to call a recess. Then they were announcing the sentence, two years, and I thought they were going to say two years periodic detention, but it was two years imprisonment. They let me and Jimi have a quick hug and then they took him away.

It gave me a sense of the power of the state that I have never forgotten. The finality of it left me stunned, how this messy, personal story, with all its backwaters and undercurrents, the teenage crush, the crying typist, the flimsy sword with its cheap metal blade, all of this had been rendered into solid objective fact, simple and final. Then I was on the number 14 bus going home to Thorndon, and I was crying, and I couldn't understand how I could be genuinely upset, and at the same time be thinking *Look at this girl, she's only seventeen years old but she's crying on a bus because her boyfriend's been taken to jail.* Part of me knew that this was the kind of thing that I wanted to happen—it was dramatic, and daring, and would make a great story later in life, when I would be middle-aged and somehow beyond all this. And I knew it was despicable to think that way, that I was such a phony.

Jimi's sentence was reduced on appeal to thirteen months, which meant he'd only serve four or six or eight—I can't remember now how the maths worked. He was at Rimutaka, and I was allowed to visit twice a weekend. I mainly went by train, then called a taxi from the Cobb & Co. at Trentham to take me to jail. I remember I left my silver dolphin rings in there one day, on the Cobb & Co. handbasin. My grandma had brought them back from the States for me. The prison had landscaped gardens, like outside some Council office, except they were surrounded by a high fence with barbed wire on top. When you arrived there was a kind of reception: you put your handbag and coat in a locker, and they searched anything you were bringing for the prisoner—I brought in books for Jimi, library books and ones I owned. The thing I remember most clearly was the doors. They were sliding panels of bars, painted a kind of beigy salmon, and just like in a prison on TV they opened in front of you and then slammed shut behind with a huge clanging noise, before the next set opened up. On my first visit I felt like looking around to catch someone's eye, as if to say *My god, how prisony is this?!*

Rimutaka was minimum security, and visiting was in a big room with other people having their visits. You were even allowed to hug when you got there. Of course, I tried to look my absolute best when I visited. The only prison outfit I remember was a woollen two-piece which I'd bought at the opshop: a peacock blue cardigan and matching below-the-knee skirt. I'd cut off the bottom six inches of the skirt, and wound them round twice to make a kind of bandage-style mini. Visiting someone in prison is not unlike other social situations, like visiting someone in hospital, or talking long distance in the days when that cost a lot of money—you know you should be making the most of your time, but it's hard to settle on things to talk about. You can't spend an hour saying *I love you.*

Because it was such a hassle getting out there, sometimes I'd do two visits in a day, and in between I'd wait in the grounds of the prison. I remember lying there on the grass, curled up in the sun with my jean jacket over my head, napping to kill the time. And there was something very weird about that time, the two or three hours that I had to pass—it stretched out in such an empty way, with the sky overhead the only thing that was moving, with clouds going past. I wonder what people thought, the prison guards and other visitors, when they saw a woman sleeping on the grass—or maybe it was normal, it was something other people did—though I never saw anyone else out there. When I think of those visits, it's that memory that comes to mind first, waiting under my jean jacket, the scraps of bright sunshine cutting through the gaps, the smell of the grass and that warm–cold feeling of being in full sunshine on a day that's probably quite cool in the shade. Maybe I only did it once. Memory has a way of turning *I did* into *I always did.*

The other thing I remember about visiting was how amazing Jimi smelled. When I came into that room, put my arms around him and buried my face in his neck, it was fantastic to get that close and breathe him in, even for a few seconds. And it was something to see the look in his eyes too, knowing what a treat I was, what a highlight. It gave you status in prison, having a girlfriend who came to visit. He must have been scared in there. He was strong but by no means prison-strong, someone who thought he could handle himself, but, really, had that ever been tested? Now he was in this place where all his talk counted for nothing, where there was violence, real violence, all the time. He got beaten up once, and they let us visit privately that week. I'll never forget the look on his face as he came across the visiting cell towards me, the sheepish smile and the big black scab on his lip, like a cockroach.

While Jimi was inside, I was selling cannabis oil that he'd made with a friend. We emptied out the powder from vitamin capsules to put the oil in—sometimes they were clear, sometimes maroon. It wasn't a very professional operation, and I had caps of oil everywhere, half-empty and empty ones knocking around all over the place.

I'd started getting a lift out to jail with a young guy I knew, and I would give him my pot tin and let him smoke as much as he wanted while I was visiting. On this day he turned up with a couple of friends, and I thought if I left my pot with him, they'd probably pressure him to smoke it all, so I gave them a couple of heads and took the tin with me. I put it in the locker in my handbag and headed in for my visit, standing at the counter while the guard checked my plastic bag of library books for Jimi. The business of prison visits had become almost normal and I waited with a sense of dull bureaucracy. As the guard moved the books around in the bag, I saw something catch his eye, and he reached in and pulled out a cap of oil—the way it was all squished you could tell it was pretty much empty—and held it up to me and said *What's this?* Everything became very slow. I felt sure I was in a dream, an anxiety dream about visiting prison. I started talking fast, of course, my answer to everything. *Oh my god I don't know what that's doing there you have to believe me I had no idea that was there why would I just put it in the bag like that I don't know where that came from give it to me let me throw it out please please just throw it away.* I was reaching across the counter to try and grab it out of his hand. And he did believe me, I could see he did—it was obvious that I wasn't trying to smuggle this near-empty cap of oil into prison in plain sight. The guard took a long look at me, then he radioed through to a superior, and said what had happened. He said he believed it was an accident, that I didn't know it was there. His boss said to call the cops.

I waited at the prison for the police to arrive, knowing that as well as the cap they'd found I had a tin of heads in my handbag, locked in the locker. Mum was overseas, so I rang my Dad, and he swore at me, the only time he ever has in anger. *Taking drugs into a prison talk about the fucking lion's den*, was what he said. When the police arrived I asked if I was under arrest and they said I was and I said *You'll be wanting this then* and handed them my tin of pot. Maybe I thought I'd get brownie points for honesty, and there was bravado to the gesture too. Even in the worst situations I indulged my flair for the throwaway line.

I was charged with possession of cannabis, and the much more serious charge of attempting to get drugs into a prison. In the end my lawyer got the second charge dropped. He got a psychiatrist's report saying—I don't know what, that they shouldn't be too hard on me— and he argued that I should get diversion a second time. When I appeared in the Upper Hutt District Court, the judge said something like *Your lawyer has done a really good job but I see dozens of young people on cannabis charges in my court every week, and I'm going to sentence you accordingly.* I got a fine of $150 and a criminal conviction. To this day, I can't travel to the United States without a visa, which can take a year to process. My parents were right: this was something I was going to regret for the rest of my life.

Being with Jimi meant going on trips to where he was growing dope. He knew a couple he'd stay with in the country while tending his patches. They lived in a double garage and had a little daughter, maybe eighteen months old. Every month, the mother would hit her own arms with gorse branches to make it look like allergies, so she could get extra money on her benefit for disposable nappies. They had two huge pet wild pigs, Jingles and Jangles, that lived in the paddock around the house. You had to put their food down quickly or they'd knock you over for it. I remember once saying something about nuclear weapons—I was working for Greenpeace by then—and someone saying *Bob Marley says have no fear from atomic energy because none of them can stop the time.* When we wanted a shower we'd go to the camping ground and feed fifty-cent pieces to the meter.

One night we were sitting around getting stoned with a guy who was quite clearly insane, a white guy connected somehow to the local Mongrel Mob. I was sitting at the table with the baby on my lap, and Jimi was sitting on the sofa with the others, and this guy was standing up, and with no warning at all he took a little jump step, swung his leg back like someone kicking a rugby ball, and kicked Jimi with full force in the knee. I became aware in an instant of just how vulnerable I was: we were in the middle of nowhere, there was no phone, the nearest neighbour was the dairy a mile away which would be closed by now. Everyone stood up and there was a bit of sort of holding the crazy guy back and Jimi walking off the pain. And then everyone settled back down in a tense affectation of normality and started watching TV again. My hands shaking, I switched the jug on, and made a black coffee, thinking if this guy comes to attack me I can throw it in his face.

After a while the guy got up and left. Our fear was

that that he'd gone up the road to get his gang member mates to come back and, I don't know, kill Jimi and rape me, we never said as much but that was what was in the air. Jimi and I were sleeping in a caravan out in the paddock, and I remember being in there, and needing to go to the loo, but being too scared to go outside, listening at every sound that could be the crunching of gravel on the road, and we were giggling hysterically, almost crying with laughter. Time passed and nothing happened. Eventually I went outside and had a piss. In the morning everything was just the same: the grass wet with dew with that countryside smell, the cold, windless air with the wire washing line, a few tea towels hanging without moving, and Jingles and Jangles snuffling around in the morning mist, their huge black forms like buffalo in the American West.

Through those friends we met Lynda, a very big trans woman and former Nomad gang member who had served time for murder, back when she'd been a man. Her boyfriend Thomas was a Jordanian from Birmingham who'd been left as a baby on the orphanage steps. Just how much of those biographies was true, who knows, but we had gotten to know Lynda and Thomas, and we liked them. She was ebullient, camp and hilarious, with an edge of menace; he was gentle, quiet, dark-skinned and balding, with curly hair growing around the back and sides. We decided to take a holiday together, and we packed up Jimi's orangy-fawn 1955 Ford Falcon stationwagon, which used to be a hearse, and headed off for a couple of days. I don't know what we were planning to do, or where we were planning to stay, but we had a fair bit of food with us, plenty of dope, and my tape deck with—I can't imagine why—only one tape, Bob Dylan on one side, Janis Joplin on the other.

It rained, and the unsealed roads got thick with clayey mud, and we weren't able to get where we were going—if indeed that was anywhere. We wound up at an isolated bach that we let ourselves into. The others went down to the beach to have a look around and I stayed at the house, grabbed a coat from the back porch as I headed to the long drop. Returning to the bach, I felt a twig or something in my hair. I reached up, felt it move and realised it was a weta. Instant panic! And no one there to help. I looked frantically around for a mirror, but there was no mirror in sight. I could feel it moving, tangled in the crown of my head. I had long, thick, curly hair well below my shoulders, a lot of it, and without thinking I just piled the hair on top of my head to bury the weta so I didn't have to touch it with my hands, and to stop it from crawling onto my face or down my neck. It was still moving, so I bent over, and put the top of my head on the bed to free my hands to . . . to do what? I didn't have a plan. And there was no way out now, the weta was so tangled in my hair I was never going to pull it out. So, with hair piled up on top of the weta, I smashed the top of my head with my fist, over and over, crushing it until I was absolutely sure it was dead. I don't remember explaining it to the others but I'm sure they found it hilarious.

We didn't stay at the bach—too scared the owners would turn up. That night we stayed in the burned-out shell of a caravan we found. It had been raining solidly for days, and everything was soaked. We went looking for firewood, but there was hardly anything—just a few sodden fallen branches, or the green wood from the bush growing all around. We were desperate to light a fire, and we worked for hours, shaving pieces of wood into shingles and slivers, propping them up around the tiny beginnings of a fire to dry out, watching them bubble and hiss with sap. And then you'd think you were really onto something, you'd be down there on all fours in the mud, blowing carefully on an ember, turning a half charred branch onto its side, watching a tiny weak flame lick up the side of a chip of wood, and some other fucker would intercede, add a branch or move a branch, blow from the other direction, or just watch and provide advice—*Oh you should move that big piece it's blocking the draft*—and then your nascent fire would flicker out, go back to just being a warm patch of damp wood and smoke and the rage! The fury! The fact that two of four of us had a violent temper didn't help.

We came to an agreement: each person would get fifteen minutes to tend the fire on their own, without anyone else watching, touching, or commenting. I can't remember getting it going, but we must have, because I have a photo in an old photo album, of Lynda in white gumboots, bending down to poke a piece of mutton in the frying pan. There's one of those speech-bubble stickers on it, remember those? They had certain comic phrases on them, suitable for any occasion. The speech bubble coming up from Lynda's head reads *IT AIN'T THE RITZ BUT IT AIN'T BAD.* Later that night, we were lying in the burned out caravan—there was barely room in there for all of us, it was one of those small 1950s caravans, no windows and no door left, but it was a roof over our head—we'd smoked a final joint, were playing some music as we drifted off to sleep—and into the companionable quiet Lynda suddenly shouted *If I hear 'Wheels on Fire' one more time I'm going to fucking kill someone!* We knew she was kidding, but we didn't play the tape again.

The next day the steep, unsealed roads were thick with mud. Late in the afternoon we got the car stuck, really stuck. We unloaded everything, stacked it up in the bush on the side of the track, and we all pushed—Jimi with his door open, the three of us at the back, the wheels spinning and spinning, covering us in thick claggy mud. No joy. We broke off branches to put beneath the wheels for traction, and they'd sometimes give enough purchase to move a foot or two, but never enough to really get going. So we gave up and slept in the car that night, Lynda in the front bench seat, me, Jimi and Thomas in a row in the back. I've got a photo of us in the morning, sitting on the back fold-down door of the car, while Jimi pushes in the end of a joint with a stalk. Lynda must have taken it. It was a sunny day, and we knew this was our big chance to get free. We couldn't fuck it up with any more half-arsed attempts. We were on a private road behind a gate that said *No Entry* so giving up and walking to civilisation wasn't an option. We decided we would have to pave the road ahead of us and we spent a good couple of hours walking up and down the track, and into the gully below, gathering rocks and fallen branches, anything solid enough to fill the muddy ruts. And then we unloaded everything from the car again, even the spare tyre, smoked one last joint for luck, and made the final push. I still remember the excitement of seeing the car finally moving with speed, clearing the end of our little paved runway and disappearing round the corner onto flatter, more manageable ground.

Adventures like this were somewhere between children's games and the adult world. I'd always loved building forts, playing war, taking risks and making myths. This wasn't so different from the Clive Road Daredevils I'd been part of aged eight or nine, digging trenches on the spare section, shoring up the walls with old pieces of wood, breaking into the abandoned flats to find an old lipstick or a poster of Basil Brush. And even the photo speech-bubbles were the same, the same ones I'd put on pictures of my friends at Lake Ferry aged eleven, running up and down the shingle dunes. That element of play was something I loved about my life with Jimi. We weren't part of the respectable world in all its boring predictability. I could still be that daring, fearless kid; only the stakes, and the company, were different.

For ten years I broke up with Jimi over and over. I had other boyfriends, was single for long stretches, and then I'd have no pot, and I'd be lonely, and I'd call him up, or go to where I knew he was, and we'd start back up again, the same tired rituals of attraction and contempt. He'd be living somewhere sad, in a damp downstairs flat in the suburbs, or a condemned house in Tonks Ave. That's where I went when I heard my friend Mark had killed himself, to Tonks Ave. I hadn't seen Jimi for ages, but I needed to get stoned, and I needed to cry in someone's arms. I turned to him in my moments of weakness, and they happened all the time, even though I was doing a lot of things right, an A student, publishing poems, getting a job. But he was always there, my rock bottom to slide back to.

The last time I saw Jimi was in a café on Cuba Street. It was twenty years ago, we'd been out of touch for years, but he recognised my car and came in to say hello. And I was shocked to see him, my heart was racing, and after some small talk I said something like, *I don't want to be rude but I just don't want to talk to you right now.* And of course he was angry, started telling me how rude that was, how badly I was behaving, and then he went out the back, to the toilet maybe or to take a table outside, and I left right away, hands shaking, because I knew that he would come back in a minute, angrier, and with more to say. Until the day I sold that car, I was always cautious about parking it in that part of town.

Even though it's the truth, it feels unfair and somehow cheap for me to write about Jimi's anger, his violence. It's like playing a card that changes the meaning of everything, makes it black-and-white. And it wasn't like that. I did so many things in that relationship that I'm ashamed of. I lied and stole and cheated, and I was cruel, and most of all I'm ashamed of how I used him, of how, over those ten years, I went back time and time again, always for the same reason. He said to me once *I don't think you really want to have sex with me, you're just trading sex for intimacy.* And I thought *No, I'm trading sex for drugs and intimacy.*

There's a photo I have of Jimi—I haven't seen it in years, but I can picture it. We were in Rotorua I think, on a camping holiday, and he's standing by the side of his dark blue car, in just his underpants. His tall, slim body is turned to the side, one leg bent like a Greek statue, and it's a boy's body really, he's maybe thirty, no chest hair, his skin taut, and there's a daisy behind his ear, not a big one, the kind of daisy that grows in the grass, that you make a daisy chain with. He doesn't know the photo's being taken because he's looking at a book in his hands, the cover just visible: *Official Scrabble Words.*

We used to play Scrabble a lot. It took forever, because he was fiercely competitive and would take so long to have his turn that by the time it was my turn I'd be sick of waiting and just go anywhere. I was a good Scrabble player, but I'd never beaten him in all the years we'd played, and it became a self-fulfilling prophecy: I didn't believe I could win, and neither did he. And then one day we were playing in the lounge of our flat. It had a gardeny damp-carpet smell because of all the leaks in the roof, and the plants to catch the leaks. I drew my letters from the tiger-pattern bag which Grandma had made for my sister to keep her marbles in. It was my turn to start, and I saw I had a seven-letter word, and I put it down, trying to stop my hand from trembling: M. A. E. S. T. R. O. *Maestro.* And Jimi challenged it of course, he was outraged, it was a foreign word, it was a proper noun, but there it was in *Official Scrabble Words,* *MAESTRO,* and there was nothing he could do about it. It was the first game against him I ever won.

A hundred
doors a night

As a canvasser for Greenpeace, your turf was a hundred doors a night. Marked on a photocopied map were your streets, with your sides of the road and cul-de-sacs highlighted by your supervisor, who would have scouted the turfs the day before. You worked in a crew of four or five and canvassed by electorate, alternating between a rich one and a poor one—Eastbourne one night, Taita the next. The best turfs were places with expensive houses, but inexpensive cars.

Our day started at 2pm with a *feelings check* around the circle of a dozen or so staff. Then we'd read out news stories, which arrived daily on some sort of telex machine, printed off in a single long piece of paper. We would share items about the ozone hole and the greenhouse effect, Japanese whaling and the Rio Earth Summit. Being armed with the latest facts would help us convince people to become members of Greenpeace, which they could do for $20 a year, on the spot, by cash, cheque or automatic payment. We never carried brochures, brochures were a loser's game. OK, we did carry them, but we pretended we didn't, and they almost never came back.

Our boss Steve had long red hair. He might have been twenty-four or so and I was nineteen but he seemed older because he was American. He couldn't understand our labour laws and would say with freckle-faced astonishment *In the States we hire people and, if they don't work out, we just fire them.* It was kind of naïve and ruthless at the same time. I learned a skill from him that I still use: when you need to cut up a piece of paper without scissors, you fold it, running your nails along the folded edge to make it really sharp; then you use your tongue to moisten the edge; and when you unfold the paper it will tear in a perfect straight line. I always think of Steve when I use that technique, his checked shirts and funny Midwestern face.

After feelings check and the news round, Steve would get us to do role plays and practice our raps. *Hi my name's Kate from Greenpeace, we're in your area tonight talking to lots of your neighbours about our work for the environment ... how do you feel about the work that Greenpeace does?* That was my standard opening. Usually, this was the first time someone had knocked on their door for a charity, apart from kids collecting tea coupons or coins for the Red Cross. *The environment* was becoming mainstream. It was only a few years after the bombing of the *Rainbow Warrior*, and very few New Zealanders will be rude to your face, so, on the whole, people were pretty friendly.

I loved being out canvassing: the cold evening air, the smell of people's dinner cooking, the glimpses into their windows as you came down the path—hands chopping at a board, a cat leaping off a bench, the light of a TV flashing against the wall. There was no one around—then as now the suburbs of New Zealand are almost entirely deserted in the evening—and it was a great feeling of power, to be the one who owned the street, who walked with purpose, who moved freely outside in the weather which always seemed so much worse to the people inside, so they'd say *Oh you must be freezing*, or *soaking*, but you almost never were. It gave me an insight into the lives of burglars, the sense of power that comes with seeing but not being seen, the voyeurism of the banal in the arrangements of people's lives: the cat bowls on their front steps, the rusted drawing pin stuck in the door. And even though it's their door that they come to answer, somehow you feel it's yours, you are the one who knocks, who rings, who creates the moment, you know who you are and what you are there for, so that when they open the door—and there is always a slight surge of adrenaline as you wait—it's as if they enter your theatre, your stage.

Sometimes you'd hit a street where the people were

just ugly, a whole street of really unattractive people. And you'd get a few doors in a row that didn't go well, and maybe a half hour would pass without you signing anyone up, or even an hour, and you'd count through your money belt and think *Shit, I've only got $34 and change and it's already 6.30 and I'm never going to make quota!* Quota was $1,600 a fortnight, so $160 was the nightly target that always loomed in your mind. If you had a good turf-buddy, they'd offer to come and do a couple of doors with you. You'd go up the path as a pair, like Mormons, and you'd just stand there while they did the door, and after you'd done a few together you'd go back to work and you'd usually do OK, you'd get a $30 at the next door, or a couple of $20 in a row, then you'd be on a roll again. The people weren't so ugly after all. They never said this to us, it was too New Age even for early Nineties Greenpeace, but every door really was a mirror.

A dog's claws on concrete make exactly the same sound as a dry leaf blowing across the ground. To this day, that particular light, barely audible clicking can make the hairs on the back of my hands stand up—a dog that isn't barking tends to be a dangerous dog. You develop a sixth sense for dogs when you're canvassing, and you get a lot of practice. You are trained not to run, you know not to run, but sometimes you have to run. I came into the front yard of a property in Island Bay once, along the main road, flat sections with flat front yards, this one had a concrete block wall in the front, about waist height. As always I made a lot of noise coming through the gate to try and draw out any dogs, whistling and jiggling the gate catch. I can't remember if I was approaching the front door or coming away from it, and I can't remember if it was two dogs or three, but I was halfway across the small yard when the German Shepherds came round from the back of the house, running and barking. I got nearly as far as the wall, but as I was about to jump it, I felt the dog's teeth grab hold of the back hem of my oversized jacket.

Your body knows how it's made and it knows what it needs to protect: the extremities are dispensable, but the torso, the neck, the head must be defended. I turned and held up my arm, holding my clip board defensively over my face and throat. The dog bit down on my elbow, and through the thick layers of oilskin, woollen lining, long sleeves underneath, I felt, not the sharp tearing sensation that I'd expected, but an incredible vice-like pressure. There was something mechanical about it—it seemed to be happening slowly, the pressure increasing with a sensation of infinite power and inevitability. Then it let go, and I jumped the wall, and that was it. The bite didn't even break the skin. But the four places where the teeth had pressed in, on either side of the elbow, swelled up like peas. I decided to go home. I must have called a taxi, but my bag was at the office with my house keys in it so I had to break in. I was halfway in our lounge window when my flatmate, a kitchen hand who worked unpredictable shifts, came running towards me with a frying pan. Jase the ace, we called him. He always reeked of designer aftershave which his school-age girlfriend shoplifted for him.

A few months later, I was canvassing a street in Karori. It sloped up, with houses on the left, a vertical bank on the right. It was the start of the night, so most people weren't at home—we'd make a note of doors to go back to later, our callbacks. The property had the look of a dog house: there was a chest-height picket fence, although no sign. I made a lot of noise as I got in through the gate, whistling and calling out, and fiddling with the latch. I knocked on the door: no reply. As I turned to walk the ten or so metres back to the gate, I heard from my left a low, steady growl. A Rottweiler was approaching slowly from the garage under the house, hackles up. With each step it put its paws down with infinite care, slow and deliberate.

It's true that when your body is flooded with adrenaline you have a lot of time to think. I calculated the distance between me and the dog and me and the gate, whether I could vault the fence or would need to open the latch, the fact that there was no one home, no one home next door, no turf-buddy or neighbours on the other side of the street. What happened next would only have two variables: me and him. I dropped into a crouch, holding my clip board up to protect my face and throat, and made appeasing, high-pitched noises as the dog came towards me with its menacing slowness. He came right up to me. I could feel his muzzle touch my body, smelling me all over, growling all the while. Sweat was running down my sides under my clothes, tickling as it ran.

After what was probably a minute or two, I started to think *I can't stay here forever.* Trying to distract him, I started to flick pieces of gravel along the concrete. Then I started to move. Every crouch-step that I crabbed towards the gate gained me about twenty centimetres. And every time I moved he would lean in from his standing position, rev his growl, and take a measured step forward. In this way, excruciatingly slowly, we got as far as the gate. I knew I would need to stand up to open it, and that the second I got higher than him he would quite possibly attack—we had learned as much in our training. But with no one around, no owners or neighbours or workmate in sight, I had no choice. As I slowly moved out of the crouch he watched and, as I got near to standing, he lunged toward me with a single bark, and I shouted or screamed back, involuntarily, and it was just enough to surprise him for a second, the second I needed to get through the gate.

The whole encounter would have lasted ten minutes, tops. I had the rest of the night to work, so off I went. It must have been summer because, when I came back down to that part of the turf to do my callbacks, it was still light. I looked into the yard and there was my nemesis, doing a shit on the lawn, crouched and trembling, comic and vulnerable.

There are different kinds of fear: the fear you feel when you're threatened by someone you know, the fear of a stranger on a dark street, all those ordinary, happy fears, of diving boards and making speeches. But the fear of an animal, an animal which could kill you, when it has you totally at its mercy, is something quite different. It smells different. When I got home that night, hours later, my own dog behaved very strangely, racing through the house whining, her tail between her legs. And the smell of my clothes in the laundry basket the next morning made saliva flood my mouth in an instant nausea.

One of the most difficult aspects of the job was needing to use the toilet. It's hard enough knocking on a stranger's door asking for money, almost impossible to make yourself ask for the loo. Also, no matter how desperate I was, I'd find that when I was signing the person up, the urge would disappear. It was only as I walked away from their front door that I'd remember. The other option was finding somewhere to go outside, but in the suburbs, leafy and deserted as they are, it's not easy. In winter it was dark early so the chances of finding somewhere were higher. I remember a house on the Kāpiti Coast: the section had a terraced garden leading down to the front door, with scoria-gravelled levels, hidden from the street. When there was no one at home I decided it was an ideal place for a piss. It was only as I came out of my squat that I moved fractionally to the right, triggering the security lights which lit up the garden like a prison yard.

A summer afternoon could be particularly difficult: hot and boring, there'd be almost no one home and we tended to be overdressed for when it would get cold later on. Bottled water wasn't a thing in those days—no one would have ever thought to have a drink with them. I remember flagging down a milk truck in Tawa—these were on the way out but you'd still see them sometimes in suburbia—and buying a bottle of grapefruit drink. Having drunk most of the pint, I was getting more and more desperate for a piss. It was one of those suburban streets with no cover: lawns in the front yards, steep gullies of bush behind white-painted railings, no sports grounds or playgrounds or local shops to offer the chance of facilities. Down one pathway was a garage built on a piece of ground dug out from the bank. There was about a foot-and-a-half-wide gap down the side of it. If anyone came down the path I'd be seen, but from any other angle I would be hidden.

My usual canvassing attire was Doc Marten boots, skintight jeans which were tie-dyed purple to cover up burn marks from drying them in the oven, and a fiercely colour-coordinated top half: a purple-and-green paisley shirt with a green and purple mohair fair isle cardigan was one of my favourite combinations. In the awkward space by the garage, I wrestled down my jeans as fast as I could and had a hasty piss. But when I went to pull my jeans up, I realised that I hadn't pulled my pants down with them, and I'd pissed all over my underwear. Panic set in as I rapidly calculated my options: unlace my Doc Martens to get my jeans and pants off, or pull up my jeans over piss-soaked underwear. With ingenuity born of desperation I had a brainwave: if I could tear through the sides of my underwear and could pull them off without removing my jeans.

Those undies were flimsy but boy they were strong! With all my strength and energy I couldn't tear through the fabric—those layers of nylon lace and elastic were just indestructible. Then, a second brainwave: my cigarette lighter. What anyone would have thought who came down the path at that point and saw a woman with her jeans round her knees, burning off her knickers, I can't imagine. But it worked, and once I'd burned through both sides I was able to extract the piss-soaked, melted undies and leave them down the side of the garage, while zipping myself back into my jeans. When someone comes to the door for charity, I always ask them if they want to use the toilet.

I canvassed for Greenpeace for two years, which meant covering all of Wellington, the Hutt, Kāpiti and the Wairarapa, twice. We'd travel too, on camping canvasses, staying in a town for a couple of weeks. In Napier, we stayed at the home of two GPs on Hospital

111

Hill. They had a lean black lab cross which we had to look after, which was easy, because it would shit on command on the dirt bank under their house. In their toilet they had a reference book of medical complaints they might come across: the two I remember were scrotum caught in zipper, and maggots in the eyes.

While we were canvassing there, someone told us that eighty per cent of the cockroaches in New Zealand had entered the country through the port of Gisborne. I'm not even sure what that statistic means, but there were lots at the house we were renting. If you bumped a painting on the wall, they'd fan out from behind it. They were big and black, maybe an inch long, and very shiny. As environmentalists, of course we looked for a natural way to eliminate them. They'd gotten into an ice cream container of honey, so we let them have it, putting it on the patio in the hope it would attract them out of the kitchen. We came home and found the dog, a Jack Russell, crunching his way through the mixture.

Nelson was a great place to canvass. You'd go up to the door of some magnificent, rambling villa with incredible harbour views, and there'd be a rusty old Nissan stationwagon parked outside—exactly the right ratio of house to car value for a Greenpeace prospect. The thing I remember best was the smell of the evening: the woodsmoke and coalsmoke that hung in the air, in a way it never could in Wellington. It made the city look like a painting of England, with its leafless trees. I knew it was pollution but it felt so right, like a wistful natural phenomenon.

In New Plymouth we kept noticing pieces of pastel-coloured gravel in people's porches. Every second house seemed to have it, a handful of pieces painted pale blue, yellow and pink, dropped by the doormat, sitting on the dirt of a houseplant or on a windowsill. Even at the house we were renting, it was scattered on the concrete patio. Just before we left town we went to the light show at Pukekura Park, and walked along the pathway under the black light. And even though we then realised what the gravel was, and knew how it would look in the light of day, it was irresistible: when you saw it glowing in that light, you had to throw it up in the air, and you had to put some in your pocket and take it home.

The workforce of door-to-door canvassers included a high proportion of troubled souls. There were young activist types as you might expect, but there were also a number of recovering alcoholics and drug addicts, and the wisdom of AA and NA mixed in quite naturally with the New Age-meets-sales-force positivity. My particular work friend was Trevor. After canvassing, we'd go round to his place and get stoned and play cards. His father had been an alcoholic, and the one thing he learned from him is that there's always a last nip of gin left, clinging to the sides, which is why you should rinse the gin bottle out with tonic.

I was also close to Shelley, a recovering alcoholic and

graduate of the Landmark Forum who smoked a lot of dope and drove fast in her dusky pink Mitsubishi Galant. In her drinking days, she'd crashed into a telephone pole at the bottom of Durham Street. When she woke up she saw what she thought were stars, but it was pieces of the windshield glittering on the road. The bottom half of her was still in the car but the top of her was on the bonnet. From time to time, she would reach into her mouth and pull out a piece of glass, which had worked its way to the surface all those years later.

Amanda was what we called in those days a *bodgie*—the term *bogan* didn't come into use until later. She was gorgeous in the way that men just lost it over: late teens, a perfect little body, long dark blonde hair, the face of a Sixties call girl, with a girl-next-door twinkle. She was soft-hearted, fiercely loyal, very funny, and all the women in the office loved her too. After we stopped working together we ran into each other on the street. Her boyfriend had been busted for receiving stolen lingerie, and while she was on the witness stand the prosecution made much of the fact that, when recovered, it was found to be 'soiled'.

By the time I left Greenpeace, I was one of the longest-standing canvassers in the country. I'd knocked a hundred doors a night, five nights a week, so in two years I must have knocked almost 50,000 doors. I'd grated the knuckle of my right forefinger cooking my first meal after moving out of home, so I always knocked with

114

the knuckle of the second finger, and I gave my knock a friendly musical rhythm: knock-knock-knock-knock knock . . . knock-knock. I had a callus on that knuckle well into my thirties. Of all those doors I remember almost nothing, just flashes: the white interior of an old woman's house in the Hutt as she showed me her family photos, the curve of a street in the hills as it started to rain. But it has given me a permanent sense of déjà-vu in the suburbs of wider Wellington. There is barely a street that I wouldn't have walked, or at least walked past, in those days, and sometimes I'll get, not a memory, but just the shadow of a memory. It's more like a flavour, a taste of the me that was there, walking those streets with my green plastic clipboard, my first job, my first taste of independence. I was so proud to work for Greenpeace, I used to wear my photo ID clipped on the outside of my backpack, so that people on the bus would know. There were so many things that were healthy about that job: the New Age positivity, the interesting people, the courage it required and the confidence that grew from it. And I was supporting myself. When I got home at night, I let myself in to my own flat with my own key. But on other levels, I was failing. I had dropped out of university. I knew I had a drug problem. My boyfriend was a dope-grower with a violent temper, and I always went back to him in the end, back to the mildewed flats, the Norse mythology and the hole punched in the bathroom wall.

In cold weather, I always wore the same jacket for

canvassing. It was an old-fashioned oilskin, the kind of thing a farmer would wear in a cheese advert, lined with green-checked woollen fabric. I'd bought it new, but over time it acquired the ancient look I'd been hoping for: battered and faded, the cuffs softened and almost worn through in a couple of places. It had big patch pockets which folded over, and I'd have my tobacco in one pocket, and my wallet in the other, the hood up. It was like a little world in there, and when I think of that time I smell that oilskin jacket, and everything it said about me: that I needed a place of refuge, that I wanted to look like I didn't care how I looked, to look authentic and eccentric and practical. And that I had rich parents to buy an expensive if unfashionable jacket, so I could achieve that look of rugged independence.

Now that I think about it, I do remember one door I canvassed, I think it might have been in Taupō. They were an old couple who had invited me in, and I would have been going on about CFCs and the ozone layer. They were smiling at me in the way that people did, people who would say I had an *honest face*, people who were just delighted to have a bright-eyed, clever young girl at their kitchen table, telling them how to save the world. They gave me a two-dollar coin—gold coins had just come in then and were still quite a novelty—but they didn't want to join Greenpeace. 'When you get to our age dear,' he said to me, 'you don't much care if the cow calves or kicks the bucket as long as it all goes quietly at the end.' She added, 'Yes, when I go to buy a new dress I wonder, will I get the wear out of it?'

Being a Greenpeace canvasser wasn't my first experience of working door-to-door. Sometimes you end up in a place, doing a thing, and it takes a while to realise that everyone there is there for the same reason: their life has gone to shit. That's where I found myself in the summer of 1991, in a motel in Te Atatū, sharing a room with half a dozen other women and selling encyclopaedias door to door. In fact, you're not really selling encyclopaedias, you're selling an appointment: as a door-to-door salesperson at the bottom of the pyramid you're there to make appointments, so your manager can go back later and *sell them in*. If they make a sale, you get $90. Of course, none of you are really selling encyclopaedias. What you're selling is misplaced hope— you're there to trade on social inequality, on the fear that comes from a lack of education, the knowledge that your children will need to work hard to drag themselves up the social ladder. You're there to find decent working people who will have just enough money to pay off the thousands of dollars, but not enough social currency to realise they would be better off getting their kids a library card.

Door-to-door encyclopaedia companies know their market, and they know their recruitment market too. The advert in the paper didn't say what the work was, maybe it mentioned something vaguely educational, but it said you could start right away, you didn't need experience, and that travel and accommodation was provided—in Auckland. This is a crucial part of the model: you never sell encyclopaedias in your own town. The advert promised exactly what I needed: to get out of town before my mother arrived back from overseas. I'd dropped out of university, my boyfriend was in jail, and his dog had just had thirteen puppies in Mum's back shed. I'd been arrested, and was waiting for a court date. I needed an escape route. So I went along to the information session for the mysterious job, and by the time Mum got back from New York I had the whole package to tell her: yes the arrest and the court date and the puppies, but I had a job, a place to live, I was leaving town, there was nothing she could do about it. Jade and her puppies, twelve bitches and a dog, with their eyes still closed, went to a farm in Tawa to be raised. I caught the train up to Auckland, making a note which would later appear in one of my first published poems: *at the backs of lives are washing lines.*

The encyclopaedia sales force included a lot of English tourists who had run out of money. I only remember one Kiwi woman, and I don't remember her story, just that in the background of it there was some violence, some kind of family abuse, and I remember feeling a shadow of middle-class guilt as I realised that some people had real problems to run away from. She had a mark on her, I seem to recall, maybe a birthmark or a bruise or a black eye, or maybe I added that in my imagination, projected it like something I'd seen in a movie.

The people running the show, the managers, were also young, maybe in their mid-twenties. They were English, but the kind of English that seemed American to me at the time, loud and brash and full of manic energy. Being put up in a hotel had sounded luxurious, but what it meant was sharing a motel unit with half a dozen other women: two sharing the double bed in one room, two in a twin room, and three of us on pull-out beds in the lounge. There was one English girl who had terrible nightmares. We'd hear about them from her roommate, how in the middle of the night she'd be kneeling at the head of the bed, screaming and clawing the wall. The Gulf War was happening at the time, and the managers especially would sit up watching it on TV and drinking. There were those black-and-white grainy shots of bombs being dropped, and when they exploded they'd cheer and celebrate like they were watching sport. Reality TV hadn't been invented then, but when I think back on us in those cramped rooms it feels like a scene from *Big Brother*: the banality, the posturing, the relentless lack of privacy.

One of the hard things about the living situation was that I needed to find a way to get stoned. I'd thought this through before leaving Wellington, and instead of bringing dope, which is hard to smoke discreetly, I'd brought oil. Cannabis can be processed down by cooking it with isopropyl alcohol to extract the oil, a brown or dark green substance that can be thick like Vegemite or more liquid like runny honey. It was usually made out of marijuana leaf—cabbage—and, while potent, it was a down-market kind of product. The best way to smoke it was with two knives heated up on a stove element: someone put a drop of oil onto the knives with a pin, while someone else rubbed the two red-hot knives together. The burst of smoke was captured, in a plastic bottle with the bottom cut off, or a glass milk bottle with a hole knocked in the base of it. But you could also smoke oil from tinfoil with a lighter underneath, sucking up the smoke with a rolled-up one- or two-dollar note. This could be done discreetly—for example, in a toilet cubicle. It wasn't a nice way to smoke—the taste of the burning tinfoil always tainted the flavour—but it was practical.

The motel had some grounds, just a bit of lawn with a few shrubs, and in the morning I would head off with my Walkman, a book and my tobacco. I'd have a couple of spots of oil and then lie on the lawn, smoking and listening to music. The evenings were trickier. Everyone smoked in the motel, so there was no pretence of going out for a cigarette. And there was nowhere to go—we were in the suburbs and there was no shop or café or pub you could even pretend you were walking to. So I'd wait until everyone had gone to bed, then pretend to have a shower. While the water ran, I'd sit on the floor of the motel bathroom spotting oil and listening for sounds of anyone coming. I'd emerge back into the faint light of the motel lounge, pick my way carefully to my bed, and lie there in the dark, heart racing with adrenaline and dope, listening to the sleep sounds of the other girls.

You sell encyclopaedias between the hours of 4 and 10pm. During the day you do training in your sales pitch. It's a tightly scripted spiel that you learn, word for word, and are encouraged to deliver with a wild enthusiasm, utterly foreign to the New Zealand way of communicating. I wish I could remember the words of the speech, but all I can recall was that at one point you were to spin around, completing a full 360, as you told the person at the door that you were talking to *all their neighbours*. The idea was that, by turning your back on them, you made yourself vulnerable, which, on a primal level, earned their trust. Given that you walked alone around suburbs you didn't know, were forbidden to carry money with you, and that this was pre-mobile phone, you were actually fairly vulnerable already. All you had was a photocopied map that showed your territory, and where you would be picked up at 10pm—usually some local strip of shops, but sometimes just the corner of a street. Although it was forbidden, I always took my tobacco with me, hidden down my pants, and I always took money, hidden in a shoe, so I could buy a bottle of Coke and sit on a gutter somewhere on a hot Auckland evening, surrounded by the yawning emptiness of New

Zealand suburban streets around dinner time. I would have knocked hundreds of doors. I don't remember any of them, just a sense of being in people's living rooms, the unfamiliar smells and the tablecloths and pictures on the wall, and being amazed at how I, a stranger, a girl not long out of school, could come into their home and take control of the situation, ask them questions and get them to do what I wanted.

Actually, there is one door I remember, a man who invited me in. I sat down for a cup of tea and a cigarette. He was fat and middle-aged, with thin hair stuck to his head. I have no idea how we got onto the subject of the occult, but I mentioned I read tarot cards—at home I had my Motherpeace deck, which had round cards because rectangles are so patriarchal. I did a reading for him with a pack of ordinary playing cards. At some point, he told me I was beautiful. That day I was wearing Levi 501s, with a white shirt tucked in, a wide black leather belt with a chunky silver buckle, and a multicoloured embroidered waistcoat, which my mother had brought me back from the US—the pattern was geometric, like a quilting pattern, and the thread changed colour as it went along. I can remember what I said when he told me I was beautiful: *You should see my sister.*

You should see my sister. It is hard to write those words. But that is what I said, and it is that moment that I remember from all the doors I knocked on and houses I entered, that combination of danger and dread, of wanting to be admired, wanting to be beautiful, being terribly lonely and in an awful situation, running away from disaster into something even worse, surrounded by careless people who didn't read and thought war was hilarious. And in the midst of all that, still being just a girl with a beautiful sister, a sister more beautiful than her, and the breath-taking vulnerability of it all, to say those words aloud, to a strange man, in a strange city.

I can't remember deciding that I couldn't do it anymore, or what lie I told the managers, or how I got to the station to catch the overnight train home. It was about two and a half weeks in, and I'd had some successful sales off my appointments, but I didn't get paid. You didn't get anything unless you stuck it out for three weeks, and I now realised what a well-thought-out rule that was. The sun was coming up as the train came out of the tunnel and we got our first view of Kāpiti Island. I was listening to *Simon and Garfunkel Live at Central Park* on my Walkman, and as we came along that coast, it was playing 'Homeward Bound'. I remember being struck even at the time by how corny the moment was, my head resting on the window as the sky got light, the dark red leather seats of the train, above me the black net of the luggage rack, the song playing, and me, the failure even at escaping from failure, not even able to last the three weeks, trying not to sob audibly as I registered the shape of Kāpiti, the silhouette which said, more than any other landscape, *home*. Mum came to meet me at Wellington

123

station. We had a hug on the platform. I wanted to cry so much, but I'm sure I didn't. She smiled at me with a look that I thought said *You idiot* and *It's OK* and *Isn't this just something so predictable?* And we walked back together along the platform. Ten days later I started my job at Greenpeace.

Foreign
body
sensation

I was standing in my boyfriend's bedroom. It had been our bedroom until I broke up with him, like I always did. There was a mirror which took up most of one wall, not in a sleazy way, just in a landlord trying to make the room seem bigger way. Out the window was the harbour, dark grey and busy with choppy waves. I was wearing undies and one of my boyfriend's pale blue shirts, brushing my hair in front of the mirror, and he said, *That shirt makes your eyes look really blue.* And I thought, *Yeah it does*, and opened my eyes a bit wider to admire them, and I brushed myself, right in the eye.

Once the shock wore off, it was like having something stuck in there, like a grain of sand. That sensation is not something you can ignore. I went to bed, tried to lie still, but it was always there, not going away, not washing out with all the tears that were running warmly down my left temple and into my hair. I'd never realised how heavy an eyelid is, how it weighs with implacable pressure and how, if you close one eye, when you look out the other side the closed eye is not at rest, but constantly held at alert, like it's holding its breath. And when the seeing eye moves, the closed one moves too, in sympathy. So, while my left eye was injured, it was also agony to open my right eye. I was, in effect, blind. Worse than the pain was the fear: not a fear of the mind, but the body's own fear, its sense that, when the eye moved around, there was something in there damaging it, cutting into its precious, vulnerable surface, and that is something the body won't countenance. Every cell of your body knows it needs to protect its eyes.

I didn't sleep all night. The room grew blue, then grey, it was morning, and I knew that I needed to get to the hospital. I never even thought to get my boyfriend to drive me—he would have been slow to leave or driven erratically, got angry at a parking attendant, or felt insulted by a nurse. It would have ended up being about him. I called my sister, and she came in her Mazda 323. Mary drove me into town and led me by the arm from the carpark and up the stairs of Wellington Hospital, telling me where the gutter was, and when a step was coming. We sat in the waiting room. A man started talking to us, and, while I couldn't see him, I could tell from my sister's voice that she didn't trust him, that he wasn't normal, but some kind of weirdo. Mary's voice had that tone, and any woman will know it, the tone you take when you don't want to talk to a man, but you also don't want to make him angry, so you don't dare just ignore him, or tell him to go away, to stop talking to you, and your scared, blinded sister. He was talking about Jesus Christ. And then, at some point, he took my hand.

Eventually a doctor saw me. They put a drop of local anaesthetic in the eye so they could get it open enough to look at, but they warned how dangerous this was, that an anaesthetised eye is incredibly vulnerable, that you could put a needle in it and not feel a thing. They examined the eye and said there was nothing in there, that I'd just scratched the surface, and it would repair itself, given time. They gave me a prescription for antibiotics, and paracetamol, and that was it. I was almost crying as I asked if there was anything else they could do, anything they could give me, because the pain, and more than that, the fear, which I'd been controlling all through that long night, I felt I couldn't endure for much longer. But they said no, just Panadol.

Mary took me home, and stayed with me, rolling my cigarettes and making my tea. I don't remember that day, just that the eye didn't get better, it got worse, much worse. It got more and more painful, and I started to have a frenzied feeling, not only about the eye, but about my whole head, a feeling that it was so painful, so vulnerable, that if anyone came near it I'd have to kill them. I felt poisoned, adrenalised, like there was something in me, not just in my eye or my head, but my whole body, that was wrong. It was a wild animal kind of feeling.

And so, maybe eight or ten or twelve hours after the first visit, we went back to A&E. By this time, according to Mary, my eye was so swollen that the left side of my face was almost as high as my nose, the lid just a line of lashes across a yellow mound. I wasn't able to open the other eye, even just a sliver, without excruciating pain. I don't know how long we waited, or if we waited, but I remember being in the cubicle—my sister was there, and a doctor, and a nurse, just voices and shapes through the cage bars of my eyelashes. And every time the doctor came towards me, even though I so desperately wanted his help, my arm would come up, like the arm of a super strength robot, to stop him from touching me—it came up with such power and speed, even though I didn't want it to. And it was funny in a way, this arm with a mind of its own, and I was apologetic and even amused, I was still myself, but my body was a different self, my body was deadly serious, and would smash against the wall anyone who came too close. Eventually, the nurse and my sister had to hold down my arms so the doctor could examine me.

They wanted to send me home with more painkillers, and more antibiotics, but this time I wasn't too proud to beg. I needed something else, I didn't know what it was, but I couldn't leave, couldn't go home again feeling like this, it was too frightening, it was a kind of insanity, being out there with the fear, and the way the fear would make the eye move around in rapid jerks, and even though I knew there wasn't anything in there, that didn't matter, because on another much more profound level I knew there was. So they agreed to give me intravenous antibiotics, and when they put them in to the fold of my arm, I could feel them burning coldly up the vein, and I felt straight away that this was better, that there was some slight tipping in the balance of power, that the terror coursing through me might be losing one percent of its domination.

At some point during this procedure, the doctor told me that an injury to the eyeball was a common cause of death in the olden days, for Vikings or in medieval times. He said it wasn't the germs from the hairbrush that were the problem, but the bacteria that live all the time on the wet surface of the eye, the aqueous humour, and that when an eyeball becomes infected, as mine had, the infection can kill you easily, before your body has a chance to fight it off, because it can travel very quickly to the brain. A scratch of a branch to the eye when out hunting, he said, and that could be it. For some reason this formed a very strong image in my mind. I saw the hunter as a young nobleman, Henry VIII–era, puffy pants and, somewhere offstage, the curly horn of the hunt. The forest around him was an English green, not New Zealand green, which is bright and yellowish, but a green that is a bit black. And when he got the scratch, it was like in an illustration of that fairy tale—it must be 'Sleeping Beauty'—when the castle gets all overgrown with thorns. It was a thorned branch like that, a thorned vine almost, which in my imagination scratched the eye of the prince.

It was Easter weekend. Maybe it was night by now. When you can't see, you lose track of time. I don't know how long it was, perhaps all of the next day and evening, but Mary stayed at my flat and looked after me. She would seat me at the table and say, the ashtray's at ten o'clock, cup of tea at two o'clock. I've always been someone who is good at moving around in the dark, and I like to think I can place my hand on anything in my home without looking—on a swimming cap, a tape measure, the stand for the Christmas tree. I was pleasantly surprised at how able I was to do things in my flat without seeing: to navigate the furniture, make my way to the toilet, and reach out my hand to the toilet roll. When you are blinded, obsessive compulsive tendencies come into their own.

The next morning I could see. The house was covered in tissues, and ash. The incredible thing about an injury to the eye is how quickly it heals. After a couple of days, there wasn't any sign of a problem, no redness, no tears, just the exquisite ease of being able to see. But some months later I woke up, and there was something in my eye, the same eye, the same place. Or that's what it felt like, the eye was running with tears, and I felt the same panic, the very logical adrenaline because, as I now knew, and my body had known all along, something in your eye can kill you in a matter of days.

I went to my GP, and he explained to me that, after an injury to the surface of the eye, even one that heals perfectly, there can remain a small anomaly in the eye's surface, a scar that is there forever, and that sometimes, especially if you're lying on that side with your face pressed into the pillow, or you don't move around a lot, or you are dehydrated, that place on your eyeball can get stuck to the eyelid, and when you open your eyes, your eyelid tears off a single cell from the surface of the cornea, and that tiny injury creates *foreign body sensation*. There is nothing you can do, just wait, because in half an hour, even less, the eye will regenerate a cell to heal the gap, and it will feel fine again. No, he couldn't give me anaesthetic eye drops, he said, they are very dangerous. You could put a needle in your eye and you wouldn't even know it.

I've experienced this phenomenon many times in the decades since. I avoid sleeping on that side, but, when I wake sometimes, I can sense that the eyelid has got stuck, and so I don't open my eyes, and I hold them still, I don't let them dart around under the lids like they want to, and then I take a little dose of courage and I screw my eyes up, like a kid when they're it in hide-and-seek. And sometimes, that act of screwing my eyes shut instead of opening them will work, and the spot will

131

unstick without damage. But other times, that doesn't work, or I open my eyes suddenly, or it's a dry room, maybe an airport hotel where I'm grabbing six hours, or I'm hungover and it's my eye's version of the dry horrors. And when that happens I get that same feeling—I open my eyes and the cell is plucked off and I have *foreign body sensation*—but now I know what it is, and I know what to do, which is just to lie there, with my eyes closed, and calmly wait. And after about ten or fifteen minutes, the cell has regrown, the surface of my eye is complete, and I can get up and go about my day.

Sometimes I worry about when I'm really old, when I'm dying. What if the people taking care of me don't understand about my eye, and they turn me over to sleep on that side because, I realise, it's not healthy to always sleep in the same position. And, more frighteningly, what if I don't know, what if I don't understand anymore what is happening, and I wake up thinking there's something in there, and I panic, or do terrible, misguided things to my eye.

It's such a private thing, the body. I mean, in some ways it's very public, or at least it's something that is known by those who are intimate, not only its appearance but its sounds, its smells, its textures. But that's all from the outside. The way you experience your body from the inside, how your tongue rests against the roof of your mouth, or the fluid ticks between your sinuses, it's so interior. For me, this regular mini-trauma with the site of my old injury is a little private drama that is played out in the theatre of my head: the physical sensations, the sense of mastery that I have, knowing how to control the situation, the undercurrent of panic that I don't allow to expand but is always there.

And of course there are the memories, of how I did the injury, the feeling of my hairbrush in my hand, and the smell of that hairbrush, of my own hair and scalp, and the pale blue shirt, the huge mirror, the harbour cut through with choppy waves, and then the man in the waiting room, holding my hand, and the house covered in tissues, like I'd been blind for a season and this was some kind of autumn. And then the discovery that this would always be with me, a phenomenon growing ever more distant from its origins, like some ancient ritual, or a children's rhyme that recalls a disease long since cured. It's a drama only I will ever know, a one-woman show, with a one-woman audience, one eye running warmly with automatic tears, while the other holds still and waits.

The Sixth
Sense

I don't remember meeting Mark. He just became someone I was aware of, living next door, tall and good looking with shoulder-length hair, some kind of artist, quiet to the point of a mental condition. All those things were attractive to me. He was living downstairs from my boyfriend, and I was in a bedsit in the house nextdoor. The night I moved in, my first night living alone, I cooked a tuna bake from the recipe on a Diamond pasta packet. Grating the cheese I grated deeply into the knuckle of my right index finger—there's still a faint, c-shaped scar there, thirty years later. I remember the sense of satisfaction though, standing in my cupboard-sized kitchen, looking out to the harbour, finally having the things I thought, at age eighteen, were all I wanted: a job, my own place, and a dog.

I got to know Mark from getting stoned together. He was intelligent, I realised, and funny, and cynical.

He was screen-printing and dyeing T-shirts to sell, supplementing his dole. He looked on my volatile boyfriend with a wry contempt, and encouraged me to break up with him, in an off-hand way. One afternoon he came up to the flat—I'd moved in with my boyfriend by then—and put my hair into dozens of tiny plaits. *You look like a model*, he said.

At some point my sister Mary and her boyfriend moved into the flat and we formed a small community, the two couples upstairs and Mark down below, and then one day Mark told me that he'd fallen in love with Mary. I can't remember what he said, but the tone was very Mark—both profound and ironic. I suppose I'd hoped he was in love with me—emotionally inaccessible, deeply depressed guys were very much my thing—but I also wasn't surprised. It seemed to me that men were always falling in love with Mary.

The flat broke up. Mary and Mark moved in together. I moved out too and went flatting with Mary's now ex-boyfriend. My boyfriend was left alone in the house, in his mind the victim at the centre of it all. My memory of the day we all moved out is of him threatening to throw my desk down the concrete stairs, then standing in the doorway, hitting himself on the head with the pipe of the vacuum cleaner. It wasn't as funny as it sounds.

I remained close to Mark during the years he and Mary were together, spending time in their succession of Island Bay flats, with their emotional dramas and painfully timid dog. And after they broke up we stayed friends. Mark was one of the only people I showed my early poems to. He never said much about them—I suppose I didn't expect him to—but I found out later he'd talked about me to his family, about my poetry and how brilliant I was.

In the summer of 1994–95 Mark and I went on holiday in Northland. His friend Matthew was living on a farm growing sweetcorn and making pottery, and we drove up there in Mark's brown Holden Camira. We were in Northland for the best part of a month, and I have just scattered memories of it now. Dangling headphones over a plastic champagne flute to amplify our tape of Billie Holiday. Mark eating muesli on the side of an estuary, his feet in the water. The pastel sunset as we came in from a swim, looking at each other in amazement, a metre-wide stingray in the water between us.

There was a shop in a tiny settlement, just a fridge in a lounge-room through someone's ranchslider, the only place for miles to buy milk. We played shuffleboard with some Germans at a pub, saying it was tradition to dance around the table with your pants down if you lost, and laughing at them as they did it. But they were full of joy, making memories, so maybe the joke was on us. We got invited to a costume party where the theme was the letter N. Matt went as a Neanderthal with the sheepskin from his car seat, Mark was Neil from *The Young Ones*, I was

Nana Mouskouri. A girl there who was rough as guts but extremely friendly insisted on giving me a sample of her conditioner, as one long curly haired woman to another. It really was amazing, and I used that brand for decades.

The Camira broke down in a tiny town called Taipa, and we were stuck there for three days waiting for our dole to go through. After we'd paid for the camping ground we only had a few dollars left. There was a local book exchange, and we'd get Ngaio Marsh mysteries for twenty cents, read them, and swap them for new ones the next day. The guy who fixed our car asked what Auckland was like. He'd never been south of Whangārei, though he did have a cousin who'd been to Rotorua once.

I remember glimpsing Mark's erection one morning in the confines of our two-person tent, a momentary eye contact but no comment made—the platonic intimacy of those moments, when we would wake together in the dawning white of the tent, or go to sleep at night, talking quietly until one of us didn't reply.

It's a long drive down from Northland to Wellington. The stereo had died so we invented a game where you take turns to sing a song starting with the letters of the alphabet. Then you do a band or a singer. Then songs with numbers. Then seasons. Then colours. Communicating with Mark was never easy, even when you were close, when you were pretty much best friends, whatever that meant. Those hours in the car together, laughing and singing, the windows down and the hot air blowing in

137

our dirty faces, are some of the most straightforwardly joyous memories I have of him.

We stopped at Taupō and slept in the car in a carpark on Spa Road. In the morning we walked down to where the thermal stream meets the river, and sat in the steaming water, like snow monkeys. I have a clear memory of walking back to the car, our earlier footprints still green against the silver grey of the dewy grass.

Make no mistake, Mark was an extremely difficult person to be friends with. He was deeply depressed, always had been, that was not news to anyone who knew him. He had talent as an artist and was studying design, but his natural inclination was always towards the darkness: to withdrawal, pessimism and self-sabotage. He picked me up one day and the car had a splintered spiderweb across the windscreen. He'd left it parked in town and someone had walked on it, he said. Later he admitted he'd punched the windscreen himself with the side of his fist, upset about god knows what. I remember visiting him at a flat in Newtown, sitting on his bed in a room with a bay window—we were talking, or I was talking, trying to spark some life in him—and just the sense of how hard it was to extract a response. It was exhausting and also came to feel humiliating. Why would you force your friendship on someone who doesn't seem to want it? We'd been friends for seven years, but I gradually saw less of Mark.

The second-to-last time I saw him was at my flat in

Kelburn. He was living in a place on the Basin Reserve by then. I don't think I'd ever been there but it sounded pretty terrible. I was in my kitchen while he was in the lounge. I was doing some job where we weren't making eye contact and Mark was complaining about his landlord. He'd put cameras in the ceiling to watch him, Mark said, and there were microphones too, and Mark would pretend to take phone calls and say things so the landlord would hear but not realise Mark knew the surveillance was happening.

Whatever I was doing, I stopped doing. I turned around to look at Mark, to see if he was joking. And the way he was saying it, it was almost as if he was joking, or at least as if he knew it wasn't true, it couldn't be true, but he was saying it anyway, sort of trying it out, maybe saying it out loud for the first time. And I said something like, *Mark, you know that's just not true don't you? That's crazy talk. You don't really believe that do you?* And he didn't defend it, but he didn't recant it either, it was somehow elided, and when I said goodbye to him that day, walked him out through the garden to give him a hug on the street, I felt really worried. Mark had always had appalling mental health, but this was of a different order, and, despite his ever-present irony, I think I knew he really did believe it. And I also felt that, by telling me, he'd been looking for something, for someone who would tell him it wasn't true, scoff at him with the blunt affection of an old friend, almost family, someone who knows you well enough never to need to be diplomatic. In the stupidly simple language of these things, it was, I think now, a *cry for help*.

I could have called the hospital, or contacted his family—he had an aunt in Wellington he was friendly with. Or I could have drawn closer to him, made more of an effort, visited him in his flat, tried to reach through that exhausting citadel of silence he built around himself, or if not reach through it, let him know, at least, that I was still there, keeping a little fire burning outside its walls. But I didn't.

The last time I saw him, he came into my work at Forest and Bird. That was surprising in itself. He rang up and said could I come to reception to meet him, he had a birthday card for Matthew which he wanted me to sign. It was the first time I'd seen him in months. He looked the same as ever, in a trench coat, with a dark brown velour sweatshirt underneath, vintage Seventies. I remember rubbing my hand against the fabric, on his chest, in a joking way, but also—to touch him. Because for all the distance that had opened between us, we were still close, still *intimates*. The card for Matthew wasn't even a birthday card, I think, it might have been a St Patrick's Day card—do I remember some tasteless leprechaun on the cover? The printed message inside was crossed out and *Happy Birthday* written in its place. And the only other thing written in there was *Sorry, Mark*.

And I said to him, *Why Sorry?* And he said, *Oh, Matt hates anyone to know when his birthday is.* And as he said it he looked at me, and the look on his face was oddly significant. It made me think there was something I was missing. But then Mark was a very cryptic person, so the feeling wasn't unfamiliar, and I just signed the card and gave it back to him. I touched his chest again and said *mmm velour* and he walked out through the glass door. That's the last I saw of him, glancing back over his shoulder.

I'd got my job at Forest and Bird straight out of university. My business card read *Kate Camp, Writer.* I'd been excited to have an 'office' of my own, a tiny room with just space for a desk and chair, but within a day of working in it I realised how unsuited I was to working alone. With no one around, the afternoon sun streaming in the window, I'd struggle to stay awake, answering resignation letters from members who deplored the roundup of the Kaimanawa horses. The first time I searched the internet was in that office. I was doing a story about the impacts of lead shot in waterways. Into Netscape Navigator's search box I typed *lead+shot* and was swamped with articles about Tiger Woods' twelve-shot lead in the US Masters.

It was early afternoon when I took a call on my office phone. A voice said *It's Mark's aunt*, and then something like *I'm afraid I have some terrible news*, but my stomach had already dropped before she said it, and maybe I said

Has Mark killed himself? or maybe she told me, and it was both shocking and the most unsurprising thing in the world.

I went into the bathroom of our office, which was a full bathroom with a shower over a bath—our building had obviously been a residence at some point. I sat on the toilet and looked at a plastic razor that someone had left on the side of the bath. I looked at the basin and the taps. The room was lit from reflected sun coming through the window behind me—a flat, greenish light, as if underwater in a shallow pond.

At some point I was back in my office and I rang my mother and she said, *Oh Kate, you were such a wonderful friend to him.*

I had only been working at Forest and Bird for three months, and, of the dozen or so workmates I had, I just didn't know anyone well enough tell them what had happened. I was broken up from my boyfriend at this point, hadn't seen him in months, but he was the only person I could cry to, and I needed to get stoned. I didn't say anything at work, just left, and went up to Tonks Ave, and my ex was there. His first reaction was anger of course, but really his response didn't matter, he was just a place of safety for me. Even though I found him and his life depressing and somehow *spent*, it was at least familiar. He wasn't my rock but he was my rock bottom and of course it was going to be there that I went.

And then I had to tell my sister. I parked on Bidwill

Street—she was flatting in a sleep-out at the back of a house there. When I walked along the garden path, I saw her putting the rubbish out, the black plastic bag in one hand suspended over the bin, the lid in the other, and I didn't say hello, I just waited for a second and watched, because I knew once I spoke, I would tell her, and then she would know, and things wouldn't be the same after that. And when she saw me I said, *It's Mark*, and she said, *He's killed himself.* And we sat and got stoned on the edge of her bed, the duvet cover with yellow stars and moons—we still have it now up at the bach but I would never choose to sleep under it. And, when I got in my car to drive away, I put it in reverse, and I looked in my rear-view mirror, and I backed up five or ten metres straight into the car behind me, just hit it for no reason, even though I saw it coming.

I went with Mary to see Mark's body at the funeral home. There was something apricot in the room. The paint? The curtains? I could hear cars going past on Aro Street. And at some point I went to his flat, with Matt, or maybe his brother. There were artworks all around, including a prominent pastel drawing of the grim reaper, his arm outstretched. There was a large bottle of Sprite in the flat and I put it by the picture, so it looked like the grim reaper was holding it, about to take a drink. *Fuck you and your grim reaper* was what I felt. *Fuck your ironic gesture.* I didn't take any of the artworks, just a lamp he'd made a shade for, and a card from a tarot deck that was there. I took the World. Again I thought, *Fuck you, I'm taking something cheerful.* I still have that card by my desk, the naked woman's body on a light blue background, surrounded by a garland of leaves.

It seemed like Mark had intended to be found on April Fools' Day, though he wasn't found until the day after. He'd gassed himself in his car, using a vacuum cleaner hose, up in the Town Belt. There wasn't a note as such, just a piece of paper with his aunt's name and address scrawled on it, as if done in semi-consciousness. He'd been drinking a bottle of whisky, and there was a packet of Lucky Strike cigarettes, even though he didn't really smoke. Matthew was prone to conspiracy thinking, but once he saw the way the car was rigged up he said he knew Mark had done it himself. Something in the bodgie effectiveness of it bore the sign of Mark's hand.

Mark's hand. We put a death notice in the paper and we wanted to say *by his own hand*, but that's not allowed. We put *suddenly and tragically* instead.

The funeral was very odd. The eulogy from the minister was pure Rowan Atkinson. *Mark*, he said, *was a painter, but in the end he painted himself out of the picture. He was a runner, but he ran away from himself.* At the crematorium the one-eyed sexton greeted us like a character in some gothic novel. We carried in the casket. The little curtains drew automatically across the opening. When we stepped outside, Matthew fell to his knees, threw his arms to the sky, howling. He said later, *A bit of drama never goes amiss.*

Matt wanted to burn the car. He got hold of it from the cops and drove it out onto the rocks at Princess Bay, where it wouldn't set anything else alight. Somehow he knew how to set fire to a car: that you need to puncture the gas tank first, drain it, and douse the car in a mixture of petrol and detergent. It was the kind of thing I would expect Matt to know, and it was satisfying to burn the car: the flames, and the anarchy of it, the sense of doing something beyond the pale.

A few days later I was back at work. My boss was an awkward man who loved nature but was not so keen on people. I remember standing in his office while he told me how elephants are the only animals that mourn their dead. They return to the place year after year, he said, visiting the bones and swinging their trunks in the dust. It was a weird extended moment that we both wished would end, but it was kindly meant.

I'd been booked to have eye surgery the day of Mark's funeral, to correct my lazy eye, and it was re-booked for a few weeks later. The innovative technique involved waking me up while a stitch was still in place behind the eye. The surgeon pulls on this to adjust the tension of the eye muscles and bring the vision into alignment. The piece of cotton was resting on the surface of my eye, and at that close range resembled one of those thick, multi-stranded ropes used to tie up ships. He came towards the eye with his tweezers and grasped the cotton, while the eyelid was held open by a steel brace, like an eyelash curler. He tugged on the stitch, holding up what looked like two fingers, but then resolved into one. For the first time since kindergarten, I wasn't wearing glasses. I felt incredibly vulnerable, the delicate skin around my eyes exposed to the air, but more than that, my eyes exposed to the unmediated gaze of others.

I can't remember when I got Mark's personal effects. It must have been a long time after because I'd moved by then, was living on the foreshore at Lyall Bay. I was told to collect his things from the Kilbirnie Watchtower—that was the gratuitously medieval name of the local police station. I only remember what was in the envelope because of a poem I wrote about it, just his wallet and a lighter, the wallet curved and moulded the way a man's wallet becomes when he carries it in his back pocket.

Grief for me wasn't sadness, it was closing down. I smoked even more pot than usual, would drive home in my lunch hour to get stoned, started drinking in the evenings too, just to switch off. Somewhere around this time I passed out one weeknight in my lounge, and took myself off to drug counselling the next day. Time dragged on. There was an arthouse film that became popular, of gypsy music from across Europe. One of the songs was played on a single wire of a broken fence, in the middle of some semi-urban wasteland, just a cracked voice and the sound of the wire being played with a bow.

It was about gypsies murdered in the holocaust, I think. Driving in my car one day I found myself humming the melody and I realised I hadn't sung or hummed a song for months.

I looked up counsellors in the phone book, and found one who listed grief among her specialities. She told me to write about the day I heard that Mark had died, and to write it in the third person. Don't focus on the things you normally talk about, she said, focus on the things you don't mention. And so I went home and wrote. *She went into the bathroom because she didn't know what to do. She didn't know anyone well enough to tell them what had happened. She saw her sister at the rubbish bin, holding the bag in her hand.*

And it worked. For the first time since it had happened, I felt compassion for this 'she', only twenty-five, losing a friend, and what does that even mean, to have a friend who kills themself, when the friendship had been drawn so thin by then, it was almost just an outline, just a few sketched marks of where a friendship had been.

In the months after he died, I often dreamed of Mark. Each time he looked slightly more damaged. In one dream, we were in a top-floor flat, sheer white curtains, light pouring in from all directions, but when I looked at Mark his face was bruised and discoloured, like the faces of people with radiation sickness in the comic book we'd had as children: *Where the Wind Blows.*

In another dream we were talking, everything seemed normal, then a trickle of blood came from the corner of his mouth.

I dreamed we were going to the movies. It was nighttime, we were walking arm in arm which is something we never did, but it felt comfortable, and we were wearing warm clothes, long outdoor coats. I had the sense of the cinema as an old-fashioned one, with red-patterned carpet like cinemas used to have. As we walked across the threshold, I looked up, and there was a sign above us, like you see in America, spelling out the name of the film in red letters on a glowing white background: *The Sixth Sense*. That was the movie we were going to see. I never dreamed about Mark again.

Why are there so many songs about rainbows?

The Peeled Banana Dance Company ran twice a week, Tuesdays and Thursdays after work, in the surf club at Island Bay. I would drive there with a friend, and we would be staggered for a moment at how lovely it was down at the coast, the sky changing colour behind the island, the fishing boats *Marco Polo* and *Gemini*, the grey-brown sand with its single line of curling surf making a sound like the tearing of an envelope. And then we'd go in and start the class, doing grapevines and box steps and our favourite, a swirling hand motion like witches whipping up the steam off a cauldron, or Kate Bush with long flowing sleeves. And after we'd practised the steps we'd put it all together as a class and perform the whole dance to a song and, as a room of middle-aged women of moderate fitness doing a synchronised dance with many mistakes, we were, we felt, transcendent: beautiful, graceful, joyous.

149

I explained to my doctor that I might have pulled a muscle at Peeled Banana. The words *groin strain* were in my mind, probably from watching rugby. But when I told him where the pain was he said it was probably related to the ovary, and he poked around my stomach and said yes, it was definitely pain in the left ovary, and it could be a number of things, but one of them could be ovarian cancer, and that was unlikely but very serious. If I could afford to go privately to get it looked at then I should, because otherwise I'd have to wait six weeks and that was not an amount of time he would recommend waiting. At some point he said that I was very calm, and I remember thinking, I don't really see what the alternative is, were there patients who would burst into tears or shriek *No no no* or say *well that's just fucking brilliant isn't it.* I said something like *Well there's not much point in getting upset at this stage.* I had a therapist at the time—she was a Scandinavian of some kind—and I remember her saying to me once, in her northern European accent, *I find it interesting that you say there is 'no point' in feeling a certain way. Do you believe that emotions should serve a utilitarian purpose?* It was the kind of annoying question you pay good money for.

When I got home from the doctor I googled ovarian cancer and found out that once you get symptoms it's usually already at stage four, and it has a high death rate, and they end up removing all your reproductive organs, just scooping you out like a fruit was how I thought of it.

I was single, thirty-six, and had always imagined, in an abstract unfocused way, that I'd have kids someday. Now I was thinking I might be dead before I'm forty.

I drove out to Bowen Hospital for a consultation about the surgery; I was on my own, never thought to take anyone with me. The surgeon explained that the biopsy might involve taking quite a bit of the ovary out, or removing the whole thing, depending on how it looked when they got in there. I would need to give consent for them to grab as much as they needed. If he removed the ovary, he said, I needed to be aware that it would be removing half of the eggs that were in my body. When you do that, the other ovary runs out quicker, so it would have a major impact on my fertility. It would be like becoming five years older overnight, he said. *It'd be like I'm 41!* I sobbed to my sister, pulled over on the roadside. Any woman in her thirties knows how huge that five-year difference would be. But of course there was no option, I needed to know if I had cancer, and if I did then having kids would be, if not the least of my worries, then certainly something down the other end of the telescope.

When I came to after the surgery, the surgeon said he'd taken about half the ovary, and, while they didn't have the lab results yet, it didn't look like cancer. It was this other non-life-threatening thing called endometriosis which causes pain and blah blah blah. I'd stopped listening. A couple of weeks later I was back at the hospital, and he explained what endometriosis is, how it gets stuck all over everything like chewing gum and keeps growing and shedding and has nowhere to go, which is what makes it so painful, because your body has no way of getting rid of it. He said mine was pretty bad, around a seven out of ten. If I wanted to have kids I'd better get onto it right away, because the endometriosis was going to make it hard if not impossible. He could put me on a drug called Danazol to stop the pain, but it would stop my periods, so maybe I could buy myself six pain-free months by taking it, and in that time I could work out how the hell I was going to try and get pregnant.

I wasn't sure I wanted kids, but I certainly wasn't sure I didn't want them. I felt like I had to try; that if I didn't there was a door that would be closed to me, and not because I'd chosen it. And I felt on some level, not fully consciously, that it would be a failure not to have children, that it would be something that other people had done and I hadn't, an experience everyone had had except me, and they would always be able to lord it over me, I would always be *less than*. It tapped into a sense I'd had of myself since childhood, of being unattractive, rejected, a *wallflower*, to use a word from our Wildfire Romance books, a word which my sister had once, cuttingly, called me as we were walking to school.

And having kids, the idea of having kids, was a kind of default setting too. Growing up we had *The Game of Life*, with its colourful wheel instead of a dice, and there were the little blue or pink pegs that you put in the back seats of the car that was your playing piece. No one ever didn't have little pegs in the back. As teenagers we'd worked out how old we'd be at *the year two thousand*. I would be twenty-eight, I figured out, and I felt quite daring predicting that, while I would of course be married, I might not have kids by then. I felt I would be the kind of progressive person who would have kids later in life, which in my teenage mind meant my early thirties. Without saying it out loud, everyone just assumed that everyone would have kids. I guess that's the definition of a social norm.

For whatever mix of reasons, I decided I wanted to try, and as a single woman of means I entered into the world of private fertility treatment. Getting approved for donor sperm from a stranger takes time, something to do with HIV testing that I can't remember the details of, but if you bring your own donor you can go right away. Time was something I didn't have, so I needed to find my own sperm. The mental list of possible people was pretty short. This would have to be someone who would do me that kind of favour, who I could cope with always having in my life, and who would be happy to be the donor, not the father. I settled on my ex, Jonathan. We'd met when he came back to New Zealand for his brother's funeral. Jonathan had been out of touch with his family for years, in a yoga cult, and then he came back for the funeral and eventually he and I had got together, and I'd been on and off my pot addiction at that time, and I'd once got so out of it I'd pissed the bed, and I wasn't sure if he was gay, straight or bi, and maybe he didn't know either, and eventually we broke up but we stayed close. All of that seemed to make him a good choice, because we'd already had some intense emotional experiences together, and he was someone who would always be in my life, who was tied to my family, and he was also someone who could deal with things by being dry and humorous and detached, which was how I like to be when confronted with emotional trauma. He said yes, and he went into Fertility Associates and masturbated in a room into a cup—they had both gay and straight porn to look at he told me, and we laughed about that. It is hard to think of a truer act of friendship.

Jonathan's sperm was approved so I went off the Danazol and onto fertility treatment. That meant injecting myself, in the fat of my stomach, twice a day, at 7am and 7pm. The device they give you is like a pen that you put a syringe inside. First you get the syringe, and you take it out of its sterile pack, and take the cap off the needle, and they teach you how to draw the right amount of hormones out of the vial, and how not to get any air bubbles in it, and then you put the syringe in the pen, and there's things you have to click and twist, and then you press it against a roll of fat, and press the button at the end of the pen, and the needle, finer than a hair, fires out into your flesh and retracts back. It really doesn't hurt at all. If you weren't looking you wouldn't even know the needle was going in. But your body has a natural resistance towards stabbing itself, so even though you know it's not going to hurt, and you're doing it all the time, there's always an adrenaline surge of fear, a gritting of the teeth to overcome it, and a relief once it's done. They give you a little yellow sharps disposal thing to put your used syringes into. And the whole process, from having the vials of hormone in the fridge, and remembering to do the injections at the right time, and handling the syringes, the unfamiliar technology, the fear of hurting yourself or doing it wrong, and the high stakes, and the secrecy, because you don't tell people you're doing fertility treatment because they say the stupidest and most hurtful things, and the doing it sitting on the toilet, because you want to be in a locked room, the whole thing is incredibly stressful. You're existing in a constant state of suspended anxiety, which you realise later is called *hope*. It's your first insight into just how toxic that emotion can be.

Around the time I started my first three-week bout of hormone injections, I met Paul on Findsomeone. On our first date we went to an amateur production of *The Darling Buds of May*. Our second was an open home for the house he ended up buying. Our third was to an underground disco night to mark the death of Michael Jackson—it was only advertised by a classified in the *In*

Memoriam column. A couple of times he'd been over at my place when I'd needed to do my 7pm injection. My small house didn't allow much room for privacy, but after years of handling illicit substances I was naturally quite sneaky, so I'd managed to smuggle my vial out of the fridge and go into the bathroom and inject myself without him noticing. We hadn't even slept together, but as it came close to the day for my eggs to be collected and fertilised I decided I needed to tell him what was going on.

I practised in my head what I was going to say. I knew it needed to be really clear, no acronyms or jargon, and I needed to remember that men generally know fuck all about the reproductive system. There shouldn't be a big preamble either. If I started with *There's something I need to tell you that I think you have a right to know . . .* he'd probably die of fright before I got to the real information. I said something like *Hey I think I should tell you that because of some medical issues I'm trying to get pregnant tomorrow by having a doctor inject me with a friend's sperm.* I can't remember what he said right away—he probably asked some questions—but what I do remember him saying was *Well, if you do it again, I hope you'd think about doing it with me.* Yes, Paul comes out of this story very well.

It turned out I couldn't have the procedure that time round anyway, the hormones hadn't worked and my eggs hadn't matured, or done whatever they're supposed to do. The fertility doctor had been asking me if I'd been feeling any side effects from the hormones, any breast tenderness, night sweats, strange emotions, and I'd been happy to report that I hadn't felt a thing. Now I was coming to realise that was a bad thing, my body's stoic insensibility. I was under-reacting, just like I always did. They said they'd change the hormones and I could try again.

For Paul and me to do IVF as a couple, we needed to have couples counselling. We explained we'd only been together a few months, and the counsellor said that could be a good thing, doing IVF placed a lot of strain on relationships, but being in the first *in love* phase might help with that, keep us connected. And it did help, I think. We were still at that stage where you've never been truly horrible to each other. You're still, to some extent, on your best behaviour. I also think doing IVF so early was good for our relationship. It forced us to have conversations in those first months that would usually take years. We saw each other cry. By the time we'd moved in together it didn't seem like a big commitment, given that we'd been trying to make a baby for the past year.

The results of the next round of injections weren't spectacular, but they were good enough for me to go in and have an egg collection. Paul came with me to Fertility Associates. The process is done with a large needle, which they put through the wall of the vagina,

157

through to the ovary to collect the eggs, guided by an ultrasound. I was sitting up on a table with stirrups I think, awake—they sedate you with one of those date-rape drugs so you can feel the pain but you don't really care, and you don't remember it very well afterwards. I just remember seeing a lot of blood on the pads on the table once I got down.

I was feeling OK, or I thought I was, or I said I was. We drove to Pranah in Newtown to get some food, and I don't remember if we ate in or took away, or how the logistics played out, but Paul had parked miles away and I had to get upset at him, to make him realise that, actually, after having a huge needle stuck through me I was not really in a state to walk to the car. And then I was crying, and it probably wasn't anything to do with walking to the car, I probably would and should have been crying anyway, because the whole process had been quite frightening, and there was so much at stake, and it was something I couldn't control, and something I was not good at, in fact my body was proving to be very bad at it, and I wasn't used to that, wasn't used to not being able to do the things I wanted, if I really wanted them and really tried. And I was exhausted, because although I don't remember it, I know I would have been so damn charming on that blood-soaked table, I would have been remarkably calm and no doubt would have commented that it was not as bad as I thought it might be, that it really wasn't that bad at all. And you have to invest a lot of energy to maintain that unaffected air.

I have always observed but am still surprised by the fact that, when you pretend to be OK, most people think you are. You're expecting at least some of them to see through you, but they almost never do.

I have a recurring dream that I am being held hostage, or in some dangerous situation, some threatening men are there who I know mean me harm. Whatever the situation, I know instinctively that the only way to survive is to pretend I don't realise they are a threat. I need to behave as if everything is fine, while calculating my escape. In one version of the dream, I am lying in bed with an intruder next to me, crouched by my face; I pretend I think he's a family member and tell him, groggily, that I'm asleep. In another I'm being held in a compound, but I walk around with my captors, politely commenting on the landscaping, while secretly looking for a way out. The dreams never resolve one way or another, but the sense on waking is of the enormous pressure of knowing your safety depends on cheerfulness, on your ability to convince others that you are blithely unaware of danger. I know my sister has the same dream sometimes.

As well as battling my under-reaction to the hormones, we had been struggling to get Paul's sperm in the system. He dutifully went into the masturbation room, with its lockable door and varieties of porn, and did what was required. Thanks for that, they said, but there doesn't seem to be any sperm in it. They recommended trying at home. The pottle of sperm could be kept against the skin, down your pants to keep it at the right temperature, and then brought in to the clinic. Again and again, Paul did the job. Again and again, nothing useful. How he felt about this process—the pressure, anxiety, humiliation—I can only imagine. I just remember the feeling of being so dependent on him, and simultaneously trying to apply zero pressure. The experience of every couple doing IVF must be different, but this part must be the same: the desire to take the pressure off each other, which becomes a kind of super pressure in itself, as each of you withholds your feelings lest you put the other one off their stride.

They weren't sure exactly what the issue was with extracting sperm from Paul's ejaculate. I must admit I was thinking *I thought there were billions of the fuckers, we only need a half a dozen!* They offered the ominous-sounding *surgical retrieval*, and Paul said yes, so the next procedure was his. I was there holding his hand while they cut open his scrotum and fossicked around in there. He couldn't see what they were doing but I could—it was like peeling the skin off a chicken leg. They would take what they got into another room to look at it under a microscope and come back in shaking their head— nothing there. They ended up deciding that Paul's sperm has this kind of condition, something you have from birth, where it never fully matures. Sperm that never grows up. I imagine it as a teenager, for some reason English, like the students at Grange Hill.

It seems horrible to say this now, but I can't even remember whose sperm we used to fertilise my eggs in the end. Was it one of the few mature ones of Paul's? Or was Jonathan's donation back in the picture? And I can't remember how many fertilised embryos we got—actually, they're not even called that: it's the stage before. They tell you how many of the eggs have been fertilised, and then they watch them, and keep you posted, as they divide from one cell into two, and then four, and then eight, and once they reach thirty-two cells they get called something else. And you're right deep in the world of it, so you know all the names for things, and the odds of things surviving, so that when you ring up for the news you know exactly what it all means. They hadn't got a great number of viable eggs from me, maybe four, and maybe they fertilised three and implanted a couple, and then it was the weekend and we were waiting to see. I had a good feeling about it. But then, I usually have a good feeling about everything, and a lot of bad shit happens anyway.

All these years later I can't remember how we got the news, just that it had failed, that those microscopic specks of hope were just . . . nothing. You can't even call them biowaste—they're just cells that go nowhere, like your body is doing all the day long, creating cells and then letting them die and sloughing them off.

Just a note: never say to someone who is struggling to get pregnant, *Have you thought about adoption?* Yes they fucking have. It's really not that easy. Not surprisingly, most babies given up for adoption have young parents, and they want their baby to go to a young couple who live on a farm and have horses and a trampoline, not a couple of sad old people living in the city. I knew people who'd done international adoption: a guy I worked with had twin girls from China, a friend's sister had adopted a Romanian orphan who was violent and disturbed. I knew I wouldn't adopt. And I knew why. It was because I didn't want it badly enough. I didn't want to run down every option, to travel overseas, get a surrogate, find a foster child. I didn't want to keep doing this. I just wanted to stop.

There are two scenes in my mind of when the process ended. I can't remember what order they came in. Paul and I are sitting at our kitchen table. It's round, but has fold-down sides, so that it can fit into the corner, and it's made of heavy parquet wood with a heavy pedestal base. I always hated that table. And I say to Paul something like, *I think I want to stop trying.* And he says he thinks the same. We're both crying. And I say, or I think, *I just can't live with the hope anymore.* Because hope has become such a burden by now. It's crushing me.

The other scene is at Fertility Associates. When I was having a smear test one time, I told the nurse that I was doing fertility treatment there. *Oh,* she said, *the doctor there is so handsome, how can you handle it?* The doctor is handsome, and he's kind, and he's a good communicator,

162

he gives you lots of information, and he doesn't talk down to you, he doesn't sugar-coat things. At the last meeting he's having with us, he's going to be giving us bad news—maybe it's about not being able to get any viable sperm from Paul, or maybe it's about our fertilised eggs crapping out, one by one, like soap bubbles popping. I'm in the waiting room reading a home magazine—it's probably *Your Home*, which is hipper than *House and Garden*, and in it there's an artwork of cut-out felt letters sewn onto a white linen cloth, all different colours of letters and it says WHY ARE THERE SO MANY SONGS ABOUT RAINBOWS. And, in what I can only describe as a small breakdown of the social contract, I tear out that page from the magazine, because I decide I want to buy an artwork like that. We used to sing 'The Rainbow Connection' at school, and Kermit sang it on *The Muppet Show* of course, and I loved the persona of Kermit when he sang, the pathos, and those skinny arms on sticks. I buy the artwork, order it from Australia, even though it's expensive, and I have it expensively framed, and every time I walk past it, for years, I get that song stuck in my head and I find myself mentally singing, at some random point of the day, *What's so amazing that keeps us star gazing*, and I realise it's been running round and round in my head since the morning. That doesn't happen anymore but for years it did. Anyway, the day I see that artwork is the day of our last visit to Fertility Associates.

No one knows we've *stopped trying*. Well, people know of course, my mum and my sister know, and my dad, and my friend, and my grandparents. They all feel sorry for us. *Enjoy life*, my grandma got into the habit of saying to me in the last decade of her life, as an imperative, whenever I would say goodbye to her. *Enjoy life*. She says it now.

Most people who do IVF don't get pregnant, but you don't hear about that much. Every story you hear is about how awful it was, how difficult, how the embryos died and the sperm wasn't viable and the relationship was strained and then, and then, it happened, and here they are, with their miracle baby, their miracle family. *I never understood the true meaning of love until I had children*. It's something people say all the time. And I always think *Yeah, fuck you too*. I mean, I'm sure it's true, but it always makes me feel bitter. I think it's because it strikes at the real heart of my fear, my grief about not having children, that there will always be some part of life—the most important, most meaningful part—that I can never experience.

For a long time, I don't like being around babies, except for the ones I know well. I hear about people getting pregnant and it's upsetting, and I hate the fact that people know that—they know that I won't want to hear it, they are protecting me, hiding the news from me, because they know I'm damaged, because I tried and failed. People mention the school holidays, and I feel stupid, because I never know when the school holidays are, am never thinking about them.

I don't like going to places where there are too many parents, because it's a community, a world, that I'm not part of and never will be. But when my nephew starts at a new school I go to his assembly, and I sit with the mothers and the fathers and the grandmas, and at one point I move to get a better view. I'm standing at the back, and he is anxiously looking for me in the crowd, and when he sees me he beams out a huge smile. Then they start, the little kids, and they're singing *If you ever find yourself stuck in the middle of the sea, I'll sail the world to find you*, and I'm trying so hard not to cry, because how pathetic would that be, to be not a parent crying, not a mother, but a childless aunt, like something out of a Victorian novel, crying as a class of other people's children sing *You can count on me like one two three I'll be there*.

People assume I have kids. It happens fairly often, and when I say I don't they go into a whole routine of how strange it is, that they would never just assume that, but there was something that gave them the impression that I did, maybe it's something I've said, or they've seen a kid's drawing at my desk or *Oh how weird I don't know why I thought that* . . . And if I like them, I rescue them. I'll say something like *Maybe you've seen me with my niece and nephew*. But most of the time I just let them flounder. They've assumed I've got kids because they do, because most people do. Or maybe they assume I've got kids because I seem like someone who understands the true meaning of love, and they're flustered to discover I don't.

Hey, I think I've earned the right to make that joke.

People who have kids think they know what it's like not to have kids, because they were childless once. But they don't know. It's different, once you know for sure, once you know you'll never be anyone's mother, anyone's grandmother, anyone's ancestor. At the most basic level, reproducing the species is the purpose of life. After my emotional grief and the sense of failure had faded, I began to experience not having children as a philosophical question. I was already an atheist, and this was like another void, another absence that threatened to suck the meaning out of life. What is the point of me, if I am not part of this primal human chain?

There isn't an answer to that of course. Or there is an answer, which is that there's no point to anything, no point to anyone. Our whole existence as a planet is just a highly improbable, unexpectable accident. It doesn't mean anything. It just is.

Years go by, friends struggle, relationships and families get damaged and break up. *Hey, people with kids are unhappy too*, I realise. So many of them are grieving for something. They have children, but there are still things missing in their lives, holes they can't fill, failures that only they know about. And I start to notice the things

I do have, especially the silences, the long, solid silences that can last for hours, the spaciousness of the days as I live them, from the orange light coming in through the pines at dawn, to the nights as we lie in our dark grey room, listening to moreporks and the tinny voice of podcasts under our pillows. *I can hear your one.* Those are the things we have. Instead of children, we have space and time. And I try not to take them for granted. And now, when I see a baby, it doesn't hurt my feelings, and I'm older now so no one says *cluck cluck* or anything else like that, and I'm not thinking, how pathetic, a childless woman who wants to hold a baby. I just pick it up and smell it, or wave at it, or squeeze its fat little arm. And then I walk away, without it.

You can heal your life

Hello, this is Louise Hay, and I would like to discuss a few ideas with you. For years, those were the words I listened to as I went to sleep, on a tape, because there weren't any podcasts then, no phones to talk to you under your pillow. *Life is really very simple,* the tape continued, *what we give out, we get back, what we think about ourselves becomes true for us.* Eventually, I knew it by heart. Not just the words, but the pauses, the intonations, the quality of her voice. There was one point, fairly late in the tape, where she stumbled over a word. I can't remember what it was now, but I always knew it was coming, and the mistake was reassuring, like a familiar hole in a tooth that you can poke with your tongue in a private act of confirmation.

In the late Eighties, a shop opened on Tinakori Road called *Divine.* It sold crystals, and dolphin jewellery, and candles, and New Age books. I'm not sure how we got on to Louise L. Hay, whether it was something Mum had heard about, or I had, or whether we just stumbled across it. But my copy of Hay's classic self-help volume *You Can Heal Your Life* has, inside the cover, in my own handwriting, *Bought for me by Mum 10/92, a gift of love.*

Now I think about it, Louise Hay and my mother are in some ways a surprising nexus, and in others perfectly aligned. My mother is unsentimental, sceptical, a member of the pull-yourself-together school of psychology. Her embrace of Louise Hay, with her wacky beliefs and Hallmark-card sentiment, was in that respect out of character. But there's a side of Hay that is about positive thinking, empowerment for women, taking responsibility for yourself. At the core of her philosophy, underlying the compassion and generosity and schmaltz, is a steely conviction that you are responsible for everything in your life. Whether it's a coldsore or cancer, a bad apartment or an abusive parent, you have created it with your patterns of thought, and you can change it by thinking new thoughts. *The point of power is in the present moment. What a wonderful thing to realise! We can begin to be free in this moment!* In some ways, then, Louise's mantras weren't so very far from Mum's own sayings: *remember who you are, the truth will set you free, stop indulging yourself.* They shared a belief that you could take charge of your emotions, and of your life, and steer yourself in a better direction. And, even though Mum never said it the way Louise did, they both embodied the belief that *deep at the centre of your being is an infinite well of love.*

169

You Can Heal Your Life is a book in three parts. Mostly it comprises a series of self-help chapters, in which Hay lays out what she believes, and gets you to do exercises, like looking at yourself in the mirror and saying *I love you*, or writing out lists of things that are wrong then turning them into affirmations: *I'm always late* becomes *It is easy for me to be on time*. Then she tells the story of her life: how she was abused as a child and adopted out a baby; how she got into Christianity then moved beyond it; how she healed herself of cancer.

At the end of the book is 'The List', in which Hay enumerates illnesses and conditions, the psychic causes of them, and the affirmations you can say to heal them. And if that condition is something like stomach fat (*I nourish myself with spiritual food*) or the common cold (*I allow my mind to relax and be at peace*) that's one thing. But an affirmation for leukaemia (*I move beyond past limitations into the freedom of the now*)? For amoebic dysentery (*I am the power and authority in my world*)? I always recognised that this list, and this whole way of thinking, is deeply problematic—actually, obscene. What is the affirmation for genocide? What was the negative pattern of thinking among the Jewish population of Poland? I knew that the Louise Hay philosophy was, at its core, unjust. It blamed people for bad things that happened to them, things they couldn't control. It said it wasn't blaming them, but it was.

And yet, the list was incredibly seductive. It had the

same allure as Myers–Briggs or a *Cosmopolitan* quiz: you could look something up and the answer was *about you*: it told you both what was wrong with you, and what you could think to make it better. And, while Louise cautioned against it, of course you used the list to read about other people, to look up their ailments and diagnose their underlying patterns of flawed thinking, and that was a way to be compassionate and judgemental at the same time. One of the main uses I made of *You Can Heal Your Life* was to hector my boyfriend about his negative ways of thinking. Eventually he too embraced the list, and its delicious blend of narcissism, self-righteousness and redemption.

But for all its flaws, Louise L. Hay's book, with its rainbow-heart cover and gratuitous middle initial, worked. I did heal my life. I did the exercises and said the affirmations. I took my child self in my arms, and released my anger into mountain streams. I embraced the practice of affirmations—one of the earliest ones I remember writing out was *I always have time for my own creative work.* This was on the back of my bedroom door when I was at university, and the same affirmation still sits above my writing desk today. And Louise Hay taught me to celebrate small victories. She'd had a client who was doing the affirmation *I am making good money being a writer*, and then, at a diner, someone came up to the woman and said, *Are you a writer?* And they asked her to write *Turkey Luncheon Special $3.95* on some pieces of cardboard, and gave her a free breakfast. That story cannot be true! Who comes up to someone in a diner and asks them if they can write? But I took on board the lesson: *When you see the first green shoots don't think, that's not enough, think oh boy here it comes.*

And every night, as I went off to sleep, I listened to the cadences of that familiar voice. The tape started with relaxing your body from head to toe. *Relax the very base of your tongue. Notice how tense your tongue was, and how good it feels to relax your tongue.* This was always the part I enjoyed the most—it seems I carry a lot of tension in my tongue. (*I rejoice in all of my life's bountiful goodness.*) A few times during the technique, you are instructed to take a deep breath. A boyfriend complained that I was always getting at him for sitting up late reading. I said I wasn't, that I would just put my eyemask on and go to sleep. *But I can hear you sighing*, he said, and I realised these were my deep, relaxing breaths. He read them as huffy, no doubt because he tended to communicate via imperceptibly subtle exhalations. Maybe that was the source of his hay fever. (*Emotional congestion. Fear of the Calendar. I am one with all of life.*)

I have such a mix of feelings about Louise Hay and *You Can Heal Your Life*. Every day I think thoughts and act in ways that I can trace back to it. When I get up from my writing desk and say out loud *Good girl*, or when I am thinking my stomach looks fat, and say *There are so many vital organs in there doing amazing things! Thanks to all you organs!* But I am also profoundly embarrassed by my connection to this book. Because it's intellectually dishonest, yes, but mainly because it's hokey. It's so eminently mockable. And if I go deeper, what I'm really embarrassed about is what it says about me, all that looking in the mirror and saying you love yourself. It says that I am self-obsessed, needy, that I'm looking for some pap to chew on with my mind, the warm glow of some happy thoughts to keep me safe in my middle-class bubble. And if I go deeper, it says that I am broken, that I am sad, that I hate myself, or that I was those things, that I looked on myself with contempt, and that I was prepared to do anything, to say anything, to swallow anything, to try and make it better.

Now go deeper, and let your skin relax. Now go deeper, and allow all your internal organs to be relaxed and peaceful. Now go even deeper, and let all your emotions . . . relax. So now, now that no one else is watching, I am going to say that my feeling for this book is gratitude. I look on it as a life raft. Maybe it was hollow, maybe it was made of plastic, maybe it was made of old chilly bins and petrol cans that were floating around, and which you can use as a buoyancy aid if you have to. You can use anything that has air in it. But that book, and the voice that I listened to in the grey light of so many bedrooms, they are precious to me. I sometimes say to my husband that if I'm in a coma, if I'm dying, he should play me the audio book of *Middlemarch*. But really, he should play me the tape. And I have no doubt that if I'm *compos mentis*, when I'm dying, it is the tape I will play in my head, that deep, resonant American voice, speaking with absolute sincerity: *In the infinity of life where I am, all is perfect whole and complete, I love and approve of myself, and all is well in my world.*

*

Louise Hay died—or 'transitioned'—in August 2017, aged 90. Her 1984 book *You Can Heal Your Life* has sold over 50 million copies.

My mother, the crime scene

The last thing I remember doing in my old life was going to the movie *Erin Brokovich*, on my own, at the Embassy. It was a Sunday night session, and the movie had only just been released, so it was packed. I'd driven from Mum's place, got a park in Mount Vic, and arrived during the shorts—hang on, we don't have shorts anymore, during the trailers. The raked rows of seats were full with people's silvery faces lit up by the screen. I had a great seat, and I enjoyed the movie. An old boss of mine had once said I reminded her of Julia Roberts. She meant because I had lots of long curly hair and a big smile, but then she got embarrassed when she remembered that, up until then, Julia Roberts was famous for playing a prostitute. Now she would be famous for playing Erin Brokovich, and when you saw the real Erin Brokovich after the movie came out, it was so disappointing.

I got woken by a phone call at seven the next morning.

It was Mum. *Hi it's me*, she said. *Now, I'm fine, but I'm at Wellington Police Station because I was attacked last night.* Did she say *I was attacked*? Or was it *Someone broke into my house and attacked me*? All I remember for sure was that she started with *Now, I'm fine*. There was almost a half a laugh in her voice as she said it, a complex semiotic device as she might say, which signalled: I am really fine and still myself, and: this situation is ridiculous, and: of course it is ludicrous to say I am fine. It was a little half breath of a laugh that said all that. And I said something like *I'll come down*. And I would have said *I love you*. And she would have said *Love you darling*.

I sat on the toilet, looking at myself in the mirror over the basin, and I said out loud *You're OK, everything's going to be fine*. I ate a banana, and put one in my bag for Mum. I got dressed in my most reassuring clothes: a pink tie-dyed T-shirt that had been made by my dead friend Mark, and a grey sweatshirt that laced at the neck, which used to belong to my sister's boyfriend. As I drove into town, the image I had in my head was of Michael Choy, the pizza delivery man. He'd been beaten and left for dead around that time, and I'd seen him on TV, unconscious, but struggling in his sleep, thrashing around in the hospital bed. Actually I must have imagined that, because surely they would never show it on TV, but that was what I kept thinking of, even though I knew Mum wasn't in hospital, that she was *fine*. I tried to picture her face bruised and damaged, to prepare myself for that, and I thought to myself: don't overreact, just be calm, she does not need anyone to be freaking out right now.

I don't remember being brought into the police station but when I saw Mum she looked OK. She didn't have any marks on her face except for one little scratch by her eyebrow, which I later found out she'd done herself, taking the pillowcase off her head. We must have had a hug but I don't remember that, I just remember offering her the banana, and she said *No I couldn't eat*, it made her nauseous to think about eating, but then she said *What I'd like is a Diet Coke*, and either I went to a vending machine and got one or someone else did, but it made me feel good, that I'd been effective. I asked if Mum had rung my sister, and she hadn't—Mary was flying out to South America in a couple of days for a three-month trip, and Mum didn't want to wake her. She'd already waited an hour to ring me because it was so early. I think I rang Mary then—I knew she would want to be there— and so the three of us were together as they interviewed Mum about what had happened.

I was in awe of the cop who did the interview. It was like a conversation, and yet the exact opposite of a conversation. When he asked questions, he gave absolutely nothing, suggested nothing. There was a neutrality to his questioning that should have felt heartless and robotic, but it was like a particularly profound form of empathy, this showing of no empathy, this asking about whether the attacker did something with his left hand or his right hand, and never saying, like a person would say: *Oh my god how terrifying.* And that was how I first heard the story of what had happened, which was that Mum had woken in the night to a masked man pushing her face into the pillow, and he asked her where the safe was, and she said *Don't be ridiculous I don't have that kind of money,* and he put a pillowcase over her head, and she pulled it off and scratched herself on the forehead, and he pulled down the bed sheets, and stuck his fingers in her vagina, and everything went blue and sparkly, and he ripped the phone out of the wall, and he tied her up and put her in the wardrobe in my old room, and he left and she untied herself and got in her car and drove to the police station and told them: *I've been attacked.*

As I recall it, the policeman was writing all this down in a hard-covered notebook, even though that doesn't make any sense—surely someone was typing it, or recording it, but I have placed in the picture a hard-covered notebook, just like one you'd have for school, a red B4 notebook with blue lines and a red left hand margin.

They were going to call the inquiry *Operation Cottleville,* after Cottleville Terrace where Mum was living. And I said, *Can you call it something else, something that doesn't identify the name of the street?,* so they called it *Operation Premier,* because Premier House was in the same suburb. I felt proud of myself for thinking of that, like I'd felt proud of getting the Diet Coke.

The next thing we needed to do was go to the After Hours Medical Centre for Mum to have a sexual assault exam. A specialist doctor would be standing by, the police said, who had a lot of experience in these exams, which are used to gather evidence. My mother, the crime scene. When we stepped onto that street between the Police Station and the library—Harris Street is it?—it was an exquisite morning, still early, not busy, and the air was so clear, the view down to the Rowing Club and beyond the harbour and the hills, even if you can't see them you know they're there, it was all so beautiful, so strange and washed clean, like the whole street, the sculpted nīkau palms and the parking spaces and the few cars moving slowly were all an hallucination, some kind of movie set. It took more than a decade for me to step or drive into Harris Street without a flash of that dissociative feeling of wonder.

I went in with Mum to the exam room with the doctor. She must have explained a lot of things, and done a lot of examining, and I suppose she was taking photographs too, for evidence. The only part I remember was her gently scraping under Mum's fingernails, like you'd clean under your own nails with a toothpick. At our bach we have a collection of swizzle sticks and several of them are shaped like little Neptune's forks, one in ruby red clear plastic, another pale blue with silver glitter. Cleaning the sand from under your nails with them gives an enormous sense of well-being. It was strange to

179

see this competent woman take my mother's hands and undertake with gentle efficiency this act which is usually one of trivial, recreational self-care.

Mum came to stay with me. I lived in a one-bedroom flat in Hiropi Street, and we agreed Mum would sleep in my bed with me. When we went to bed, I expected her to be awake in the night, like my vision of Michael Choy, I imagined her calling out in her sleep, writhing and thrashing. But she went to sleep in a few minutes, with the radio on like she always did, and she slept through the night. I was the one who was awake, listening to her breathing, trying not to roll over too much, wishing I could turn the radio off but knowing that, from now on until further notice, Mum needed to have everything she wanted, needed to have things her own way. My job was to act normal, be present, and help. The next day the police came around, and they asked Mum what she wanted from the house. She couldn't go in there, they said, while it was still a crime scene. So she told them where her undies were, and the other clothes that she wanted, and they went and got them for her.

Mum was insistent that Mary should still go on her trip to South America—she didn't want *that bastard* to ruin that—so we saw her off at the airport. Mary and I were both crying, Mum wasn't, and I could tell she didn't appreciate the drama.

I don't know how long it was until we could go back into Mum's house, but she was determined to move back there, to live there alone again, even though they hadn't caught the guy, and so one day, after a week or two or three, we went back, for Mum to move back in. I don't know what I was expecting when we stepped back in through the kitchen door. I'd lived there for years so it felt like my home too. It was all so familiar: the stairs from the car pad and the way you turned the door handle. It had been a magnificent house, owned by an interior decorator, a very *House and Garden* type of house, steeped in history, with its kitchen bench salvaged from some historic school, and its outside light from the *Wahine*. But as we stepped into it that day, even though it looked the same, it felt different, like a spell had been broken. Everything in it that was ordinary, imperfect, or worn you saw for the first time. It was *diminished*: just a house.

I think I stayed there the first night with Mum, but maybe she didn't even let me do that. She was resolute about living there alone. Every night before bed, she would go through the house, checking every door, looking in every cupboard, even opening the oven to check in there—*That's how I know I've gone mad*, she said, *because I check inside the oven*. But I understood. Back at my flat in Newtown, I had discovered a new moment of terror I'd never known existed. It came between the time when I switched off the light, and when my eyes adjusted to see in the dark, just a second or two when I couldn't see anything, and every night it gave me a surge of panic. My bedroom light was on a string hanging from the high ceiling, and I can see myself now, having pulled that long white string until the light clicked off, standing frozen, braced, before my eyes adjusted and the streetlight slowly dawned in the room as an orange-white glow. My heart rate would eventually return to normal as I lay in bed, listening to affirmations on a tape: *Hello. This is Louise Hay and I'd like to discuss a few ideas with you.*

The same thing happened to me, for years, when I took a top off. For the moment I was there with a T-shirt over my head, not able to see around me, I was terrified.

There was media coverage of the attack of course, and they wanted a comment from Mum. I was able to help again. I told her to say she would do written answers to written questions. She didn't have to talk to the journalist. She gave an articulate, staunchly feminist comment, exactly the kind of thing they weren't looking for, no doubt, but they printed it anyway, something about it being an attack on all women. It was of course. Every woman was frightened by it, especially the ones who lived alone.

We heard more from the police about what had happened, and every new detail was awful. He had unscrewed the bulb in the security light. He had tried every window and door, eventually using a crowbar to prise open the kitchen door, just splintering the lock out of the wood. He had spent a long time in the house, had moved some pictures in the study, maybe looking for the imaginary safe. One of these pictures was the framed book cover of my first book, and that has always scared me, because I know he's seen my name and photo, that he knows who I am. The mask he was wearing was actually a scarf from inside Mum's house. He'd taken some scissors and made eye holes in it. That horrified Mum, because the scissors were in the drawer where the knives are. There was the *Sabatier knife* in there—a phrase from my childhood: I never knew why but I knew it was a special knife, and a special word, because it was French, and Mum would always pronounce French words with élan.

The picture that built up was of a man determined to get in. There was no element of opportunism, no door or window left unsecured. He had spent a long time in the house, probably hours, while Mum was asleep upstairs. And at some point we found out that they had collected cigarette butts from the dairy across the road, which had a small seating area outside it, because they thought he had sat there, maybe weeks in advance, watching the house.

One of the ways people respond when they hear about terrible things is to immediately think about why this couldn't happen to them. They don't know they're doing it, it's just a reflex. And so in the aftermath of Mum's attack we heard uncountable times about the alarm systems that people had, monitored around the clock, the security locks they had on their windows, about their dogs, their husbands, their drawing of curtains and use of security chains, their choices to live where they did, their neighbours close by. And then there were the people who just couldn't face Mum, knowing what had happened. People would avoid her on the street, she said, avoid her eye. And there were people who saw Mum, and knew about it, but didn't mention it, because, let's face it, none of us is experienced in saying *Oh hi, I heard you were the victim of a home invasion, how are you?* And of course Mum wasn't acting the way you're supposed to act. She wasn't weeping with dignity in a hanky. She was brittle and angry, impatient, forgetful, irreverent and jumpy as hell. So when people did talk to her, she was likely to say something they didn't know how to handle, because it was harshly funny or intentionally blunt, designed to stop them in their tracks. Being the victim of unimaginable horror is a kind of a superpower, and like all superpowers it leaves you very isolated.

When I was little, I had a book about learning to draw. You started with a basic shape, in this case an oval, and added or took away elements to create a drawing. From the oval you drew a birdcage. I showed Mum how to do it, but, instead of a birdcage, she turned her oval into a man with a mask over his face. *Mummy's droing* she wrote in the corner—she was all about subverting the dominant paradigm. It's only when you're traumatised by a man wearing a mask that you realise how often this image appears in our visual culture: a bank robber in a balaclava, a terrorist, maybe a policeman responding to an armed offender, even a scuba diver—any image like this would send Mum into a panic. She was—is—drawn to read about rapes and murders. When a new one happened I would tell her not to follow it, but she wouldn't be able to help herself. I would ring and say something like *There's a programme coming on about the Parnell Panther, you need to not watch that.* And she would say *oh god,* and then *yes yes yes* with an eye-rolling sound. Sometimes she would do what I said and not watch it, sometimes she would watch it, and then be haunted by every detail and say later, *You were right, I can't watch those things.*

The masked invader. That was what Mum called him. I found it irritating, like a malapropism of masked intruder, but Mum is a language person and I knew it was important that she get to define the terms, so I called him that too. Years went by and they didn't catch the masked invader. Mum sold her house and moved to one with views down through a valley of pine trees to the harbour. It was modern, steel and glass, the kind of house she'd always wanted.

The police kept in touch with Mum. They put a new detective on the case, and we went in to see him so he could explain where things were at. I remember being awed as he gestured to the files around him, shelf after shelf of thick Eastlight ringbinders, all relating to the case. The guy they suspected was a serial offender. They believed he'd attacked a woman in Aro Valley, and he'd been found there another time, in another woman's garden. He'd attacked a woman in Kelburn, tied her to her bed, broken her jaw. He'd broken into a house in Newtown and they looked for his car on the red-light camera, watched hours of footage, and they'd seen it, too blurry to read the number plate but it wasn't a common car so they thought they had something. Who knows when we heard all this, how the information dripped out to us over the years of their pursuit, but each morsel of information would require hours of analysis as we pored over what we'd been told. And of course each detail set off a whole new reel of imagined horrors, of what it would be like to be tied to your bed, to be hit, to be left for dead.

Our encounters with the police were like a form of existential therapy. It was a comfort to know that the state, this objective machinery, was there, that they believed this mad mad story, and that they would use their alien attitudes, their precision and thoroughness and unimaginative dogged tedious attention to detail, their conformism and rule-following and conservatism, all of the things we didn't value, all of that they would use on our behalf. Mum had been anti-police since the Springbok Tour, and I was too, as a druggie and a liberal. We were embarrassed to find how we worshipped them now, how we carried their cards in our wallets as talismans, and played the part of grateful women, protected by the patriarchy.

I'm shocked to find I don't remember getting the news that they'd caught the masked invader. He had hundreds of convictions, we found out, for all sorts of stuff. One way they'd identified him as a suspect was noticing that the series of attacks had stopped when he was in prison for something else. At first he denied everything, which meant a court case, but eventually he pleaded guilty. I went on my own to the High Court in Molesworth Street for the sentencing. I didn't know what it would be like to see him there, would I be frightened or angry, would we make eye contact. Would he do something, laugh or speak or make some outburst? He didn't do anything; he just sat there, looking the same as he would in the paper the next day; he looked scary. And he was older than you would expect, as if attacking women in their sleep is something you should grow out of.

The judge's comments were fantastic. I knew Mum would be happy to hear them, about how he had planned and premeditated his crimes, how he'd victimised women, how he was a disturbed individual who posed a great risk to society. The tone was that the judge had his number, knew exactly how dangerous he was, that he wasn't taken in by any of his bullshit. He gave a sentence of preventive detention, the harshest sentence you can get in New Zealand—it means you can be kept in prison indefinitely, until the Parole Board thinks it's safe for you to come out. There was a non-parole period of eight years, but after he said that the judge said something like

Make no mistake, preventive detention is a life sentence. It was as much as we could have hoped for.

As I left the court I was approached by a reporter from TVNZ. I still see him sometimes on things, his gelled blond hair like the washed-up drummer from a New Wave band. He asked what my connection was to the case, and I said I was a daughter of one of the victims. Would I like to talk about it on camera, he asked. They could disguise my voice and appearance, and I pictured myself for a second, in profile and in shadow, my legs crossed, while a garbled version of my voice explained how terrible it all was. But Mum had always said to us, even as children, apropos of nothing, *Never speak to the media.* And I didn't.

The next day, there was a big story in the paper about the masked invader, the crimes he'd done, his unusual childhood, the way the houses he'd chosen looked like the house he grew up in—he was attacking his adoptive mother, the implication was, and it was probably true, but on another level I felt like, let's leave his mother out of this.

Life improved with him locked away. I still felt scared when I walked to my front door in the dark, but I could talk myself down. It was the same for Mum: her conscious mind had some counter arguments to her primal fears.

A big part of how we responded to the attack was how we grappled with the sheer unlikeliness of it. If you know anything about male violence, about sexual assault, you know it hardly ever happens this way: a random attack by a stranger. You're way more likely to be attacked by a man you know. The masked man in a woman's bedroom is a staple of popular culture but in real life it's very rare, like being struck by lightning. And then it happened, and we were left with a sense that anything is possible— and not in a good way, *anything is possible*, it meant even your most irrational fear could come true. So I knew it was crazy to think the masked invader would break out of jail and come to get me, but then, it was crazy to think that he'd seek out the imaginary safe of an English teacher in the grey pre-dawn of historic Thorndon, that was statistically so improbable it made no sense, and yet it had happened.

Nine Eleven happened the year after Mum's attack. From my flat in Hiropi Street I'd see planes coming in to land, disappearing behind the pines on Mount Victoria as they descended towards the airport. For weeks, months after, if I saw a plane coming in I'd always flinch as it reached the hillside, because they looked like they were flying straight into it, because that was what could happen, we knew now, what could always have happened: planes could fly straight into things while everyone watched them do it.

When you're the victim of a serious crime you are enrolled on the victim notification register. When anything important happens, like the offender is coming up for parole or gets moved to a different prison, or if he dies—dreams are free—you or your designated person will get notified. I was the designated person for Mum, and so one day I got a letter in the mail saying that the masked invader was coming up for parole. Incredibly, eight years had passed. We were offered the chance to make written submissions to the Parole Board, and to appear before them, and we said yes, we wanted to do both.

In some ways I relished the opportunity. It was something I knew we would do well. And there was a vindication to it, a satisfaction in being able to articulate exactly what we knew: *he thinks he's a burglar but he's actually a rapist, he is a sick person who is a danger to all women.* But it was an awful thing to do, too, because we knew he would read these submissions, would get the satisfaction of knowing how he'd damaged us, knowing how, like the sad whimpering women we didn't want to be, we were afraid to sleep alone, afraid of the dark, afraid to pull a T-shirt over our heads or open the pantry door. We knew we needed to show the Parole Board how our lives were broken, but we had put so much energy into being OK we didn't want to parade our losses to the world.

And on a primal level, even though I hate to admit it, as I wrote my submission I was scared. Scared to make him angry. Maybe when he got out he'd come after me, throw my words in my face, rape me or murder me in revenge.

In the end I fell back on what I knew about writing, which was that you can't think about the audience, whether they're a reviewer, a relative, or a rapist, all you can do is write the truest thing you can. *Never apologise, never explain* was another one of Mum's sayings from childhood. So in the end I wrote my submission to the Parole Board as honestly and straightforwardly as I could, and I said that I was scared, and that Mum was scared, of being attacked by the masked invader if he ever came out, even though I hated to admit it, and to put ideas in his head, to tempt fate in that way, but I put it down anyway, and we sent our submissions to the Board.

If I say to you, *appearing before the Parole Board*, you're probably picturing a wood-panelled courtroom, high ceilings, robes and wigs. But of course, like so many of the most awful things in life, the Parole Board takes place in an environment of banal bureaucracy, in a low-ceilinged meeting room between Lambton Quay and the Terrace. The Department of Corrections—a name both twee and Orwellian. First you get buzzed into the glass door to reception, the only sign you're in a place to do with violence. You wait on the chairs which are a few inches lower than you expect them to be, so you always slightly fall into them. And you're in your work clothes of course, it's the working day. My sister and I are wearing our favourite work clothes—we want to be on our fashion game on Parole Board day—and Mum is dressed more casually: as usual she doesn't have a handbag but carries her keys and purse in her hands, a trait I find particularly irritating, in the way only something your mother does can be. Then the receptionist takes you through, and you walk into a large meeting room, and the Parole Board members stand up and shake your hands. They're a bunch of older white people, four of them I think, usually men though there is the occasional woman. They're judges, ex-cops; one's a psychiatrist and that person's usually our favourite, because he's not part of the machinery of state—our late-life love for the police is still balanced against our distrust of the patriarchy. We sit down opposite them, Mum in the middle, my sister and I on either side. Everyone introduces themselves, and there's a lot of solid, middle-class eye-contact and rueful, lips-together smiles.

For many years we are fortunate, because the Chair of the Parole Board happens to be the judge who sentenced the masked invader, and he knows very well just how psycho he is. Mostly the members of the Parole Board are pretty good listeners—that's what they're there for after all—but sometimes they feel the need to patronise, to interrupt, to explain the blindingly obvious, even to correct or question some assumption that one of us may have made. I regret to say that one of the worst at this is a rare women on the panel: she interrupts Mum a number of times, misinterprets her, goes off down a rabbit hole explaining the law when of course the law doesn't matter, explaining things to us doesn't matter, that's not why we're here. We are here to be heard, not because we think it makes any difference, although it probably does, but we are here to be heard for a simpler and more profound reason. It is an act of faith, of superstition really, that we would always do whatever we could to keep him locked up so that, when he does come out, it will not be for any lack of trying on our part. I will go to the Parole Board every time until he dies, or I do. And I'm sure that after they release him I'll be able to keep going, because he'll offend again, and get caught again, and then I'll be there in a told-you-so capacity.

I hear my sister and my mother talking. We all sound so alike that when we lived together no one could tell us apart on the phone. I can hear the tremor and emotion in their voices and in mine as we speak, but no one else would notice it. And then it's time to leave, we are getting up and pushing out our chairs from the grey formica table, and we shake hands on the way out the door, and we're in the lift, laughing about the Board members, the ones we liked and the awful ones, and recapping what they told us about the masked invader and his so-called progress. Usually we go for a coffee afterwards. We have always been a family that kisses on the lips, so when it's time to go back to work, for Mum to go home, we kiss each other goodbye on the lips, my sister's and my mother's soft, dry lips. Mum isn't wearing a jacket, as well as not carrying a handbag, so she's got no pockets, and as she gets on the bus, has her keys in her hand and her purse tucked in her armpit. Maddening!

The Parole Board usually makes its decision that day. The Department of Corrections calls and says parole has been declined. That's what they've said so far, every year. Sometimes it's two years between hearings, which is great, but it still comes around quickly, the letter in December, when things are getting busy for Christmas, and the hearing in the New Year. And Mary or I, whoever is registered as the victim contact, has to get in touch and let the others know it's that time again. *Motherfucker*, we say, that literal motherfucker is up for parole again.

He gets some day releases now, to go to work. They had to let us know that he'd be travelling in to Wellington on the train, and walking to wherever he is working. He's not allowed to go anywhere else along the way, and he's not allowed to access the internet, or do some other things, there are other things he's not allowed to do, I guess waking women up to finger fuck them is included on that list. He's electronically monitored the whole time, they assure us in the letter, and if we have any questions we should ask, and we do, we ask a lot of questions, and they answer some of them, and some of them remain unsatisfactorily mysterious, there are blank spots in our knowledge, and it's always going to be that way because you can't know everything and even if you did it wouldn't help. But it's like opening the oven door: it's something you still need to do.

A path
to victory

Our bathroom had dark blue wallpaper with birds and
flowers on it, like the wallpaper in an English country
house. The paintwork was putty-coloured, with a putty-
coloured bath shelf that Dad had built for Mum. As
well as room for Mum's mug of Nescafé, it had a sloping
holder with a lip to hold her book, or the latest issue of
the *Bulletin*. Once I was having a bubble bath with a jar
of hard boiled sweets on the shelf, and Dad called me
a *little sybarite*. In the bathroom cupboard was a wide-
mouthed orange plastic jug. Its lip was shaped like an
upper lip, with a cupid's bow. This is the jug Mum would
use to wash our hair, and as I write that I can see my
sister's fine, straight hair being washed with it, hanging
down her back while I sit in the bath behind. I used to
like to force the jug under the bathwater, filled with air,
then let the air out in huge, transparent bubbles.

This is my first memory of American politics. I'm not

sure where they come from, but I am in our bathroom and I have a sheet of satirical stickers about Richard Nixon. They are the kind of stickers that are cut into shapes, and when you peel them off they will leave thin, odd-shaped pieces of blank white sticker behind. And I don't think I know who Richard Nixon is, but one of the stickers has the phrase *BUM'S RUSH* on it and it shows Nixon in a hurry, with those speed lines and a cloud of speed dust behind him. Maybe it says *Tricky Dicky* on there too, or maybe that's something I've heard my Mum and Dad say, or maybe I'm pasting that in now, from the present day, when I'm someone who has taken a great deal of interest in Richard Nixon, who has even seen the door that was broken into by the Watergate burglars, the door itself, and the piece of Sellotape they used to hold the lock open. Mum says that she remembers those years, being at home with us as babies, praying that she would live long enough to find out what really happened with Watergate.

My next American politics memory happens in a toilet as well. The public toilets near our bach were a favourite place to play: the cool shadow in the heat of the day, the concrete block walls you could climb up on and crab around, the excitement and mystery of the Men's with its gurgling dark-silver urinal and luminous chemical-smelling *toilet lollies*. There was always graffiti scratched into the back of the toilet doors: love heart, initials, *4 eva*. I'm not sure what inspired us to take our crayons down to the toilets and do our own graffiti, but

196

I do remember what we wrote, not least because it was there for years afterwards. There was the misspelled *Poo to yuo* just inside the entrance door, and then, which must have been mystifying to read, in child's printing and at child height, *Down with Reagan*. This would have been the summer of 1980, with Reagan about to be inaugurated, but at the Waimeha Stream public toilets we were keeping the Carter dream alive.

Our biggest political statement we saved for the wall facing the entry. It was a phrase that captured another important cultural battle as the Seventies transitioned into the Eighties. With some signwriting flair, the first words were written title case along the top, with the final word in all caps, as tall as we were, thickly gone over with all the colours of crayons and supplemented with multiple exclamation marks: *I Love Disco YEAH!!!* A few supporting comments that *Disco's not dead* were scattered about on the concrete-block walls.

I retained into adulthood a love of disco, and of American politics. At the time of the Clinton impeachment I was in my twenties, living away from home, but Mum and I were still close and we followed it avidly. As feminists we felt quite good about taking the unusual position of not despising Monica Lewinsky. But we didn't judge Bill Clinton harshly—we reserved our hatred for Linda Tripp, the bad friend who taped the late-night phone calls and told Monica to keep the blue dress. A few years later, we followed *Bush v Gore* too, taking inordinate pleasure in enunciating the words *hanging chads*.

I was preparing to review *To Kill a Mockingbird* on the radio the week that Obama won the Democratic nomination instead of Hillary Clinton. Few people remember that the famous courtroom scene in *Mockingbird* turns on a woman's false accusation of rape by a Black man. As I talked about the book—which I do love—there was a twisted through-line there for me: how the patriarchy sets its enemies against each other; how, somehow, for a Black man to win it has to be at the expense of a woman. And I was excited for Obama to win, of course I was, but there was Hillary, soldiering on in her pant suit and pearls, bearing all the scars of a thousand unfair attacks and having, yet again, to be a good sport, humiliated, overlooked and not even allowed to be angry. I remembered a bumper sticker from the 90s: *Impeach the President: And her husband*.

Around that time I joined the dating site Findsomeone. I was explaining internet dating to Mum, and I showed her my profile which said *I must admit I like geeky guys who know a lot.*

What do you mean know a lot? Mum said. *Know a lot about what? It really doesn't matter*, I said, *I just like guys who know a lot of stuff. But like what?* Mum said, and she wouldn't let it drop, so I said, *I don't know, they can name all the presidents of the United States or something*. She seemed happy with that answer.

In total I dated eleven guys off Findsomeone. Most were just one-off coffee meet-ups, with neither party following up. Even as an extrovert, they were uniformly awkward and nerve-racking. I met number eleven, Paul, at the Krazy Lounge. It was a cold day, and my nose was running, but on the plus side I was wearing my favourite shirt dress and a badge that said *I Miss Helen*. I looked in through the window and thought, that must be him, wearing a shirt with the sleeves rolled up, and a woollen vest, and glasses—a Kennedy cabinet type, I said to Mum later, meaning attractively nerdy and old-fashioned, with an air of a thoroughly decent fellow.

It must have been three or four dates in when Paul invited me round for dinner. I sat with my feet curled up on an armchair, while he cooked in his cupboard-like kitchen. The flat was horrible, a breeze-block unit in a mouldy part of Karori, but I could tell he'd made an effort: he was cooking from a Nigella cookbook and there was even a tablecloth. There were some videos on top of the TV, and he put one in the machine for me, saying something like *This'll give you a laugh*. As the picture jerked on, I recognised Pete Sinclair, host of *Mastermind. Paul Mulrooney, university student from Dunedin, your subject is Presidents of the United States of America and your time starts now.*

His back-up topic was Watergate.

I don't remember Hillary announcing her run for President, just the sense of dread: the knowledge of her imperfections, the shabby history—Whitewater, Benghazi—her paranoia, the care she took with everything, how wooden and studied she could appear, and how her competence, her diligence, her seriousness would become a liability. Her age, her experience, everything she had needed to have a chance, everything she had been forced to do, every box she'd had to cut off limbs to squeeze herself into, would now be held against her. She was too old, too boring, too moderate. She was corrupt, tainted, uninspiring. And wasn't it just creepy to have a President who'd been married to another president, like a dynasty, like the Bushes.

And of course she was not the candidate any of us, any woman, any feminist, would dream of. But I was still all in. As a younger woman I'd seen her as my mother's generation, but now, in middle age, I identified with Hillary. And I was so angry at Bernie. Because it's easy to be the guy who sits at the back of the room and yells things out, while at the front is some harried, over-burdened woman, the one who has to actually make things happen, who doesn't get to have funny clothes and an old-person face and still be popular.

When Hillary won the nomination, Mum and I decided to go over, *to see the first woman elected President* was how we always described it. It never occurred to us that she could lose. Along with my now-husband Paul, we planned a trip to Boston, New York and Washington. As a surprise for Paul, I booked our final night, election night, at the Watergate Hotel, which had been recently renovated and re-opened. It was our first, freezing-cold morning in Boston when I broke the news to him that we'd be staying there. I don't think I've ever seen him more excited.

The trip naturally encompassed some political sightseeing. In Boston we Ubered out to the Kennedy Presidential Library. The best thing there was the coconut he had written his plea for help on, when his boat was marooned during World War Two. The coconut reads: *NAURO ISL ... COMMANDER ... NATIVE KNOWS POS'IT ... HE CAN PILOT ... 11 ALIVE ... NEED SMALL BOAT ... KENNEDY.*

JFK swam three miles to the island, towing an injured crewmate by holding the strap of his lifejacket in his teeth.

In Washington we went to Ford's Theatre. Plays are still performed there, and there was someone up a ladder, fixing sets or lighting on the stage. Looking in to the box where Lincoln was shot, standing where John Wilkes Booth had stood, I had for the first time a sense of the assassination as a murder: sad, sordid, intimate. Across the road they have a bed with a blood-stained pillow, where Lincoln was taken and died. I can't remember if it was real or not. At the gift shop we bought miniature busts of the Presidents and an Abraham Lincoln magnet saying *Tall Skinny and Honest.*

All year I'd been following the election build up: the

primaries, the debates, the grab them by the pussy, the basket of deplorables, Donna Brazil's debate questions, John Podesta's risotto recipe, Ted Cruz's father and the Kennedy assassination; we were bursting through new thresholds of crazy on a daily basis, and that hadn't become normal yet. The campaign felt like an out-of-control fairground ride: no matter how bad it got, how much damage it did, how sick and terrified we felt, it would eventually stop. All we had to do was hang in there, and come November 8 it would all be over.

Election Day dawned beautifully crisp and clear. I put on my newly purchased Ann Taylor wool-blend motorcycle jacket, my blue striped scarf, and my badge that said *I'm ready for Hillary*, and we took a last walk around the leafy neighbourhood. The streets of terraced houses led on to city blocks, and we were stunned to see a line of hundreds upon hundreds of people, and realise they were queuing to vote, under trees flaming orange against the blue sky. It was both shocking and moving. Most of them were young, but I saw an older Black woman there with her adult daughters, telling them they were going to wait with her for as long as it took. Everyone looked like they were voting for Hillary. They probably were—Washington DC is overwhelmingly Democrat. Despite the Comey letter, despite the whole misogynistic sick bag of it all, I felt optimistic. As we walked back to the apartment, I saw a rat, standing on the marble side of the Dupont Circle fountain, drinking from the water. It was surprising and disgusting and exhilarating all at once—I always feel that way when I see rats in a city—it's so *overseas*.

It was time to decamp to the Watergate. Apart from its political history, it's an iconic building architecturally, its curved black-and-white layers unique in a blocky city. There isn't much around that area, no shops or cafés, but we didn't care: our plan was to stock up on snacks and watch election coverage all day, until Hillary won, when we'd go for a drink in the hotel bar. At reception we got the key card that said *No need to break in*, and immediately souvenired the in-room pencil that read, in gold print: *I STOLE THIS FROM THE WATERGATE HOTEL*.

Underneath the building was a small cluster of shops, including a number of empty ones. There were a travel agent, a hair salon and a convenience store, not a 7/11—not a chain store, but the kind of shop that seems oddly temporary, as if someone had some boxes of junk food and a carpeted office space and thought *Why not?* We bought Frito Lays and Cokes and lollies and headed up to our room. The beds were enormous, two huge California Kings, three pillows wide. The view out the window was of the Potomac river, misty, with a mix of autumn colour and winter-bare trees. Mum had a Hillary T-shirt and we took pictures of each other, making the muscle arm pose. We agreed we'd go for a drink at 9pm, or when Hillary won California, whichever came first. We settled in with Wolf Blitzer and CNN's interactive map.

Everyone knows the feeling, the slow draining away of hope. It happens in sports matches, and in real things too—waiting for the phone call that never comes, realising that if you haven't heard by now you haven't got the job, won the prize, been asked on the date. We were texting with my sister in New Zealand, and my only positive memory of the night is hearing that my nine-year-old nephew was telling her authoritatively: *If Hillary wins Wisconsin she still has a path to victory.*

We never went for that drink in the bar. At midnight, Paul and I went down to reception. The two staff members on duty, one Black, one Hispanic, were watching the coverage on the reception desk computer, one seated, one bent over the other's shoulder. Suddenly I felt ashamed of myself. We would be getting on plane the next day and leaving all this behind, but how terrified they must be. Like us, they still weren't quite convinced it was over, hoping for a miracle that never came.

I had called in to Radio New Zealand the night before to talk to my friend Bryan Crump about the US election hype. Now I stayed up until 1.30am, for another update. Was there a phone in the bathroom, by the toilet, à la Elvis? Or did I stretch the hotel phone in there? Either way, I sat on the marble floor and talked to Bryan. I was tired, and shocked, but it felt good to have something to do, a chance to try and make sense of it all.

I'd said to him the night before that Hillary reminded me of that saint, I couldn't remember which one, the one covered in arrows. She was so damaged and scarred; she was dragging behind her all the hatchets and knives that had been stuck into her over the years. Hillary wasn't perfect, I'd said to Bryan—she was, in many ways, toxic—but maybe that was what it took for a woman to become president, like the uranium-tipped bullets that can pierce armour. But now I knew she hadn't pierced anything. At her New York venue, under the largest glass ceiling in America, her supporters were crying.

The next day was our last one in the US. We decided to stay in our room until Hillary gave her concession speech. It was going to be at eleven o'clock, then at twelve, then at one. We waited. When she finally spoke, Paul and I were sitting on our bed, but at some point I moved over to Mum's, so I could cry in her arms. It was all so shocking, so surprising, yet so predictable. And among all the different intermingled forms of despair was the feeling that, while there might be a woman president in my lifetime, maybe there wouldn't be in Mum's, and even if there was, we wouldn't be there in the Watergate together, to look at each other and experience that moment of history.

It felt good to be leaving the country. At the airport souvenir store there were T-shirts for sale saying *Don't blame me, I voted for Hillary*. I desperately wish I'd bought

205

one, but at the time I was just too heartsick. I thought I would never want to think about this moment again.

We arrived home on a Friday. It had been raining all week. On the Saturday morning, our neighbour came round to say there'd been a slip down the front of our houses. It probably wouldn't affect us, he said—not a great comfort given we are perched on a vertical hillside, cantilevered out into the tree tops. On the Sunday, late at night, we felt the house shake and rumble. In the dark we could hear things smashing. We both jumped out of bed and stood in doorways, even though that's no longer recommended, now they say if the earth is shaking just stay in bed, do nothing, pull your pillow over your head and hope for the best. We imagined our house sliding down the bank. *Abbotsford* was the word in my head. The shaking stopped, and we found out it was an earthquake. The house wasn't slipping away. Not yet anyway.

Four years of the Trump presidency showed us that time doesn't heal all wounds, or even wound all heels. When the assault on the Capitol happened, Paul and I were at home with our new puppy. Like many awful things in life, like the whole Trump fiasco, what was happening at the Capitol seemed ridiculous and impotent at the start, then grew into something frightening. One piece of footage I kept seeing showed people walking slowly within a path defined by a velvet rope. One man was moving the stanchions holding the rope back a foot or two, to widen the pathway. It took me a few days to discover that these were people walking into the Capitol, not filing out of it. The lack of urgency, of fear, the sense of banal entitlement, was astonishing. Apart from the flags they were carrying, they didn't look that different from a normal tour group, shuffling along, every second person filming things on their phone.

Two weeks later, we got up to watch the inauguration. I don't really care about Joe Biden, and I'm not a fan of inaugurations, can't stand the formality, the Bible holding, the speeches filled with abstract nouns. So I was surprised to find that, as Biden took the oath of office, I was crying. Not welling up, not choking up, but red-faced, cover-your-mouth-with-your-hand sobs. *It should never have happened*, I said to Paul, *it was a terrible thing.* For a moment I allowed myself to grieve for everything the Trump era had destroyed.

I'm up here at the bach now, looking out over the toilets. They've been painted in recent years with a mural showing dunes and waves. I don't particularly like it, but I know that's because it's new. I want the toilets to be unpainted grey breeze blocks like they were forty years ago, when I declared my support for disco along with my American politics.

There's a small cabinet here filled with the kind of stuff you find at baches: old scrapbooks of kids' drawings, a bowl of shells, a hand-held fan in the shape of a unicorn. On the end is a bumper sticker: *Hillary President 2016.* I don't remember buying it on that US trip, but I'm glad I did. It'll be here for decades now, and when my nephew is my age he'll remember the family story of how he sat up as a nine-year-old on that election night, and thought Hillary had *a path to victory*. The day of the Capitol riot he posted on Instagram: *Just wtf America*. And on inauguration day: *Finally, democracy prevails*.

Surface
Paradise

At Waikanae we sleep on bunks. I am a top-bunk child, having always been drawn to any element of risk or novelty, while my sister prefers the closed-in privacy of the bottom bunk. She lies on her back and pushes against the mesh with her feet, bouncing me on my upper bunk; the sound of the metal squeaking and straining. Our sleeping bags aren't padded, just a cream flannel liner, and a thin polyester outer—mine purple, Mary's orange. In the very early morning, once the sun is up, we go out onto the lawn in our sleeping bags, the smell of the grass and the early morning air and the sun, as it gets warmer, the smell of the sun on us, on our bodies and our sleeping bags and our night-time-smelling pillows. They say smell is the last sense to go when you die, and I would like that to be the last thing I smell, that memory smell of an early summer morning on the lawn with my sister, Mum and Dad and our black lab Sheba still asleep inside.

When I was in my twenties, the bach got rented out. Lots of the stuff we used to have got thrown away, or lost, or it got stolen by the girlfriend of our tenant—he was very depressed and she was, our mythology has it, a kleptomaniac who stole all of the forks but none of the knives or spoons. She stole our cane hanging chair—the property manager went round and saw it in her garage, but she wouldn't give it back. Another tenant got behind on the rent so Mum kicked her out. The property manager took the tenant's side. *She is devasted*, he said in a letter. We always say *devasted* now instead of devastated.

Still, I can go into the memory bach anytime, and recover items that are no longer there, that I haven't seen in decades. The stand-up vacuum cleaner, with its brown cloth bag and H. O. O. V. E. R. written down it vertically, the noise it made, and the feeling you'd get as you looped the cord around the cord-holder. There were plastic plate-holders in the shape of fish, which were never used but were always there, tucked on top of the half-size hot-water cylinder. There was a tiny glass with hand-painted flowers around its base. When I dropped it to the floor and shattered it, in my thirties, I was *devasted*.

Most precious of all was the monster puzzle book sent over from America by our Uncle Adrian. In our cardboard box of comics under the bunks, among the issues of *Archie and Jughead*, *Betty and Veronica*, *Whizzer and Chips* and *Beano* and *Dandy*, it was the only thing that was constant, that was never replaced by a new edition, a new *Double Digest* bought for us on a trip to the bookshop. I can't remember what the monster puzzle book was called, or even the cover, but I remember two spreads within it. The first was a zombie supermarket, where the undead pushed carts around the aisles. The other I recall with an almost spiritual longing. The page was dark, black-and-red, and the maze was of a pyramid, where mummies roamed the subterranean chambers, which glowed golden yellow. Each one of the mazes, no doubt, had been traced years before, but the book wasn't there to *do*; it was there to look at, and maybe not even to look at; it was there to revert to, to go back to, a faith object, this limp-covered novelty book, probably picked up at the counter of a *grocery store* at Halloween.

In those days the TV at Waikanae sits up high, by the roof, on top of the cabinet that holds Mum and Dad's clothes and that their bed slides under during the day. And the TV has its own curtain that you draw across in front of it, so burglars can't see it I guess. It's a black-and-white curtain with blobby patterns—I recognise them now as Marimekko style. Next to the TV is a kind of wall that isn't a wall, just a downwards beam and a crossbar, and then an open doorway, more a gesture of a wall, and on the crossbar is where we put our nativity scene, which is maybe six inches high and made of brown plastic, with all the nativity figures moulded inside it, and one of them has broken off and been glued back with a visible blob of Araldite. And the big Santa Claus candle goes up there too on the crossbar, which is how Mary pulls it over and spills hot wax on her face that seals her eyes shut. One day there's a tsunami warning and Dad gets up onto the crossbar and pretends to be a parrot. That is the best day.

When you have dinner at Waikanae you have the deer antler knives and forks—they're all rough like the bark of trees, except for one fork which is smooth and Mary always likes to have that one. Waikanae plates are plastic—there are the big orange dinner plates, and the small plates and bowls are different colours; one of the bowls is dark blue and has got a bit melted by something, but that's still my favourite. There's a tiny teapot that Dad makes his tea in, and a mug he always drinks it out of which is yellowy brown and looks like it's woven out of flax. Mum has her royal mug, from the Queen's coronation. She's drinking from it ironically, I know that even as a child, even though I don't know the word. I know that Mum doesn't really love the Queen like the mug thinks she does.

Sometimes we have a fondue, which smells nice because of the meths that's burning underneath with a blue flame you can hardly see. It might be a cheese fondue that you dip bits of bread in, or a chocolate fondue. There are six red fondue forks with different colours on the end. Sometimes we use them to toast marshmallows on the fire. Mary takes ages carefully getting her marshmallow evenly tan on all sides. I generally let mine catch on fire, then blow it out, and eat the black, carbonised crust and the molten interior.

Hanging up in the rafters there's a huge sombrero, and the top of it is all frayed, so that when you lie back with it over your face in the sun you can see the sky through that hole while you smell the straw that it's made out of. My uncle's surfboard is there too. Dad ties it up with yellow rope after my uncle comes back from Darwin where he's been building houses because of Cyclone Tracy. Also up there in the rafters is our kite, right at the peak of the roof, hanging in the dark against the dark wood. It's dark blue and dark green, sort of cellophane, with a semi-circular shape, and it has eyes I think, with blue and green streamers that dangle below. Maybe it's a jellyfish? When Dad flies it at the beach, he sometimes lets us hold the string, and you can feel it tug against your hand. He's trying to get it flying, and it's circling and crashing around down at ground level, and then it's flying, and it gets so high so fast. Dad likes to joke around that he's lost hold of the string, which is attached to a piece of driftwood; he pretends he's dropped it and it's bumping along the sand and then he chases it while we're screaming, and Dad has such long legs, only a few steps of his will let him catch it, and reach it with his long arms. And then one day he's doing it, he's pretending to lose hold of it, but this time he doesn't catch it, and our kite blows away—it flies out towards Kāpiti Island until it's just a dot, and then, nothing.

213

When you go to the beach for a swim you've got a towel wrapped round you, though you're probably not lucky enough to have the best towel, which is Mum's and which is agreed, by unspoken consensus, to be the greatest towel ever seen. It's black. There's a show stopper right there, a black towel. And it has white fringes at the ends, like the fringes on a sun umbrella. At one end there's a yellow pineapple embroidered on the towel, as big as your head, and in cursive script, embroidered in white, *Surfers Paradise*. I've heard this place talked about before, and always heard it as *surface paradise*, so I think that *Surfers Paradise* is a play on words which makes me love the towel even more. I once wrote about this towel and a workmate got in touch to say his family had the same one as a kid, and he felt exactly the same about it, and he didn't know where it was now. Cash paid for this towel. Please contact the author.

When you go to the pool you'll take a towel, a big colourful one that has a nametag sewn into the corner of it, and when you come out of the pool you'll lie on the hot concrete with the towel completely over you, and from that dark shelter you'll look out onto the splintering bright light of the world, the screaming and so bright blue of the pool, but you'll be focused on the little pebbles set flat into the concrete, and how you can put a drip of water onto one of them, from your finger or from a piece of your hair, and watch it evaporate off the hot surface. One moment the pebble will be dark with water, then

214

the dark will start to shrink and fade until the pebble is dry again. I went to that pool recently for the first time in decades. As I stepped into the changing rooms, I felt myself there again in my tiny body, always so impatient to get dry I'd be pulling my knickers over half-damp legs, that uncomfortable grabby feeling. And then the sense of well-being that comes from rolling your togs up in your towel forming a tight, neat roll. I once informed a stranger in that pool, pointing to my grandmother, *She can't put her head under and she's older than I am!*

Mum and Dad spend lots of time reading library books and drinking black coffee in the hot sun. Their bed is in the lounge, and you might pass Dad, sitting on the edge of the bed in his undies, gouging at a verruca on his foot with a plastic cocktail fork. If we go out somewhere, Mum might be wearing her strapless dress that has elastic holding it up at the waist and under her armpits. In the car she will pull it down to flash her breast at us, to send us into a frenzy of embarrassment. Sometimes she gets food colouring and dyes the potatoes blue or green.

The only time I remember my parents having a fight was at Waikanae. I don't remember the fight, just that Mum gets so upset she says she is going to stay in a motel, and she gets in her car and drives away. Mary is in the bunk room and Dad is reading to me from *Monkeys of the World*, which has a monkey on the cover with a big distorted-looking nose. Everything feels strange because Mum has gone off and only Dad is there, but I pretend things are normal by looking at the monkey book. Later Mum is there and she says she only came back to wash her hair. Even I know that's not true.

One day I'm down at the beach playing in the dunes with my friend. We're in the lupins with their yellow flowers and rattling, furry seed pods, probably playing shops, pretending a log is the counter and paying each other in seeds and leaves. A man walks up to us and says, *Have you ever seen a man wink before?* That's not what he says of course, but that's what I hear. And then I notice he has something pink in his hand, and I realise it's his penis—he seems to be sort of rolling it between his thumb and finger. In any emergency I know that the most important thing is to act like everything is normal, and I also know I should make him think we're not alone, so I say something like *Did you see the holiday programme down on the beach?* And I keep talking on, about the holiday programme and what a nice day it is, and eventually he walks away.

We go home to our own baches. I know that the man has done something bad, even if I'm not quite sure what it is, and I know that I should tell Mum and Dad, and then they will call the police and the police will come and find him and get him into trouble, but in the end I don't say anything, because for once in my life I can't think of what to say, I literally don't have the words to describe what has happened.

There's hardly any hot water at Waikanae because of

216

the tiny hot-water cylinder. When we're little we have baths in the *shub*, and when we have chickenpox we sit in there in a lukewarm bath of calamine lotion. I might be in the bathroom having Solarcaine sprayed on my back after I've got sunburned, or be in the bunkroom in my togs while Dad's putting Coppertone on me from the big copper-brown bottle. Mum loves the sun and always gets sunburned despite her olivy complexion. Mary and I compete to be the one who gets to pull *the peel* off her back, using both hands to try and pull away as big a sheet as we can of the fragile, translucent skin.

We go down to the dairy to get bread wrapped round the middle with a white piece of newsprint. Mary can carry the money and Kate can do the talking. As we get older we steal money from Mum's purse or Dad's change from his pockets, and we buy miniature sacks of Gold Rush bubblegum, packets of strong-smelling Hubba Bubba, grape and original, and Big Charlie in a long rope. Our jaws are constantly working and Mum and Dad tell us to chew with our mouth shut but we don't.

In 1980 we got Raleigh Twenties for Christmas. They were identical green ones, with just a slightly different diamond pattern on the white vinyl seat. We learned to ride the usual way, Mum and Dad pushing us from behind on the grass. Training wheels weren't really a thing as I remember it, and even if they were, I sense they would be the kind of thing my parents would disapprove of, like driving barefoot or having your ears pierced.

The driveway of our bach was short with chunky gravel. I rode down the driveway, not quite in control, across the street, and hit the kerb, landing on the footpath on my chin. The next thing I remember is being in the back of the car, with a plastic bowl on my lap to catch the blood and broken bits of teeth. How typically heartless it was of my parents, I thought, to worry about the upholstery.

I had my chin stitched up at the Waikanae medical centre. The anaesthetic meant it wasn't painful, but I could feel the tugging as the cotton went through. I was surprised to find that they sewed up a face with what looked like the same cotton you'd use to sew on a button. The next memory is the smell of the chemist shop: that mix of the vaguely medicinal, perfumed soaps, and no doubt some bags of potpourri. I got to choose a cuddly toy from the chemist, and although I was going to spend the next three weeks eating only mashed foods, and the next several months having regular trips to the dentist, the toy I chose really almost made it all worthwhile. It was two dogs, one fawn, one a warm rusty brown, with long arms that locked them in an embrace, and paws that velcroed behind each other's heads. I called them Romeo and Juliet, and even years later they retained a faint trace of the chemist shop smell.

Sometimes at Waikanae we have to go to bed while

it's still light. And then sometimes Mum and Dad will wake us up later, and take us for a *midnight walk*. I don't know if it's actually midnight, but it's dark, and there's no wind. We get dressed and go down onto the beach. Earlier in the day Dad has made a fire down there, and he lights it, and once it's died down a bit we put bananas wrapped in tinfoil into the embers.

It's surprising how much you can see once your eyes adjust to the dark. The beach is like the surface of the moon. The sand smells different, has an almost burnt smell, resolutely neutral, and there's so many stars, way more stars than you see in Wellington, they go all the way down to the sea. The cooked bananas don't taste that great, but they're hot, and they've been cooked on a fire on the beach. I suppose we eat them with a spoon, but I can't remember that, just the sight of them as they come off the fire in their blackened, wrinkled tinfoil, like some lunar explorers rescued from a crash site. Maybe this only happens once, the *midnight walk*. Maybe everything only happens once.

Acknowledgements

I began this book on the Katherine Mansfield Menton Fellowship in 2017, and I am very grateful for the support of the Katherine Mansfield Menton Trust. Thanks to Te Papa for giving me time off work to finish it in 2021.

I wanted this book to be as honest I could make it. I'm sure there are things in it that are wrong, in lots of different ways. Everyone's memories are different and these are just mine.

It's not easy for my parents, Michael Camp and Elaine Lynskey, to read a book like this. I hope it's obvious that I love them very much.

Dad says it wasn't him who let the kite go, it was us kids, to make him chase it along the beach. That sounds about right. He can't understand why there's so much bad stuff in this book, when I have had so many successes along the way. Dad is proud of me and only sees the good. Thanks Dad.

Mum let me write about her attack and was surprised at how staunch she appears. I wasn't surprised. I have always been inspired by Mum. She used to ask if I was writing any poems about her and I'd say *only the one 'My mother fucked me up and I never forgave her'*. We find that very funny. It's a bit weird to say, but I think Mum and I are actually soul mates. Thanks Mum.

My sister Mary is the person who knows the most about me. Every time I sent her an essay from this book she'd send back emails that just said *CRYING*. She's the closest thing I have to another self to help me go through life and make sense of it. Thanks Mary.

I feel that my husband Paul Mulrooney comes out of this book very well. I wouldn't have had the courage to go back to some of these memories without him here to anchor me in the present. Thanks Paul.

Thanks to my friend and ex-boyfriend Jonathan Pierce for letting me invade his privacy and portray him, if not awash in my urine, then somewhere close to it. And to the wider Pierce family, I hope that my memories of Mark add to yours, and that you know I think of him with love.

When I wrote the chapter about the attack on my mother, I remembered the support I had through that time from three wonderful women, Pinky Agnew, Vivienne Plumb and Caren Wilton. They let me laugh and complain and say the unsayable—what a gift.

The cover photo was taken by Dionne Ward at Te

Papa and I'm so glad I could get permission to use it. Thanks to Ebony Lamb for the author photo.

Mary Karr's book *The Art of Memoir* was a big help when I was getting started on this project , and I am grateful to Catherine Chidgey whose insightful cheerleading was a confidence boost in those early stages.

A final thank you to Fergus Barrowman and the team at Te Herenga Waka Press. I am so lucky to have been publishing for 25 years with this stellar bunch of people.